THE SELLING EDGE

Winning Over Today's Business Customers

Michael Levokove

with Celeste Levokove

THE
SELLING
EDGE

THE SELLING EDGE

Winning Over Today's Business Customers

Michael Levokove

with

Celeste Levokove

Glenbridge Publishing Ltd.

Library of Congress Catalog Card Number: LC 92-75676

International Standard Book Number: 0-944435-21-1

Printed in the U. S. A.

CONTENTS

Preface

This book emphasizes the specific skills that will be required by business-to-business salespeople over the next decade.

Throughout this book I will refer to a Top Performer (TP) and an Average Performer (AP). These salespeople are composites of the many people, male and female, whom I have known and observed in my business career. They may be selling fiber optic products, electronic cash registers, or payment processing systems. They may be located in New York, Boston, or San Francisco.

I will also make occasional reference to "systems selling." Success in systems selling, much like consultative (A.K.A. benefit and/or added value) selling, depends on one's ability to sell solutions to business problems, not product/service features. The techniques used in systems selling can be applied to many business-to-business sales situations, from turnkey software packages and computer systems to the sale of advertising, engineering, accounting services, and medical or electronic equipment. Selling cycles can be long, sometimes longer than a year.

The examples used come from personal experience or from the experiences of my peers. Names have been changed to protect the privacy of individuals. However, I have worked for and with some of the companies mentioned and considered it important to retain those company names for credibility's sake.

Introduction

Pick up any newspaper or magazine and the headlines tell the same story.

Restructuring/Downsizing

- "For most, a leaner structure means not only increased workload but also diminished chances for promotion, and the frustration that fosters."[1]

- "Firms Values Seem to Shift As Lean and Mean Wins, Big Happy (Corporate) Family Loses"[2]

- "Many industries are restructuring top to bottom to shed debt, to adjust to a new era of low defense spending and to meet tougher competition in the global marketplace of the 1990s."[3]

[1]Carol Hymowitz, "When Firms Cut Out Middle Managers, Those at Top and Bottom Often Suffer," *The Wall Street Journal,* April 5, 1990, p. B1.

[2]Allen Murray and David Wessel, "Torrent of Job Cuts Shows Human Toll Of Recession Goes On," *The Wall Street Journal,* December 12, 1991, p. A1.

[3]Robert A. Rankin, "Stable rates mask broader crisis," *The Denver Post,* February 23, 1992, p. 3H.

Overworked

- "Blame it on the brutally competitive economy that forces us to take on heavier work loads."[4]

- "With fewer managerial bodies left those left often end up working harder and longer."[5]

- "Even survivors aren't secure; many must work longer hours amid more (corporate) belt tightening."[6]

Stress

- "For many, stress is simply the by-product of working in a more competitive world."[7]

How does all this impact you?

In the worst case scenario, it could cost you your job. At the very least, you will be looking at less support, cutbacks in training, and heavy competition for the few promotions that will exist in your organization. No doubt, you will be expected to do more with less.

Business customers are demanding more from you too. Due to the competitive nature of the marketplace, they know they can. They aren't just looking for a supplier of a product anymore. Today they are expecting you to function as their

---

[4]Gordon Williams, "Flaming out on the job," *Modern Maturity,* October/November 1991.

[5]Anne B. Fisher, "The Moral Crisis," *Fortune,* November 18, 1991, p. 71.

[6]Thomas F. O'Boyle, "Fear and Stress in the Office Take Toll," *The Wall Street Journal,* November 6, 1990, p. B1.

[7]Ibid.

business partner, a partner who searches for ways to help solve their problems.

So where does all this leave you? You're stretched to the limit, and the last time you looked, there were still only twenty-four hours in a day.

First, you have to recognize that the business environment has changed, and it will continue to impact your selling efforts. Second, you cannot depend on your management to give you all the support and training you're going to need in these tight times. To ensure your chances of success, you are going to have to rely on yourself.

So how do you survive and, more importantly, how do you succeed in this new business world? With limited time and increasing demands, you'll have to do a better job of planning and sticking to your plan. You will have to maximize your "on-the-road" time and be able to qualify your customers faster. You will have to position yourself as a problem solver and quickly determine your customer's business problems. In short, you will need to become more skillful in all aspects of the sales process. To become more skillful you must re-examine everything you do—from the basics of how you develop your revenue plan and map out your territory to your methods for closing and servicing an account. To succeed, you will have to recognize the qualities that constitute top performance and then understand how to incorporate those qualities into your sales activities.

Your role model, Top Performer (TP), will illustrate the value of planning and what constitutes a good plan. Through TP, you will be given practical suggestions on how to maximize your customer face-to-face visits and techniques to determine your customer's real business problems. Further, you will begin to appreciate the value of the consultative selling approach and how it can sharpen your proposals. Lastly, TP will guide you through objection handling and demonstrate a simple and effective technique for closing.

The Selling Edge

We will identify what skills management considers essential for promotion and then lay the groundwork to ensure your success in sales management once promotion occurs. We will illustrate how to avoid many of the common sales management pitfalls and demonstrate how you can build a highly motivated sales organization.

PART I

HOW TO BECOME A TOP PERFORMER

1

WHAT MAKES A GOOD SALESPERSON FOR THE '90s?

"The best salespeople are extroverts."

"Well, I don't know if I'd use the word extrovert. An extrovert makes a lousy listener. He never finds out what the customer really needs. Let's just say the best salespeople are friendly, sociable, and outgoing."

"Okay, I agree, but you don't want them too-too sociable. We're talking business here. I want my salespeople remembering what they are there for. They can be Mr. Sociable on their own time. What I need is a salesperson who's professional."

"I think we can both agree on that. The best salespeople are professional and have strong technical skills."

"Hold on. Who are you kidding? Technical people never know when to ask for the order. They get too wrapped up in details. No! I have to disagree with you there. The best salespeople are definitely nontechnical!"

Put two managers together and the debate could go on forever. Each could make a case for the desirability of a particular personality trait in a given selling situation. The truth of the matter is that the best salespeople are extroverts, friendly, outgoing, reserved, technical, and nontechnical. Good salespeople come from all backgrounds and fit all personality profiles. The one and only indisputable fact is that the good salesperson is the one who succeeds.

3

Given the same desire to succeed, why is it that certain salespeople consistently meet or exceed their quotas while others, working just as hard or harder, always come up short? What differentiates that Top Performer from the marginal salesperson?

The Top Performer

It has been my experience that the Top Performer sets himself apart in four major ways:

1. He understands that success is dependent upon his ability to manage the sales process efficiently. It is also important to note that the Top Performer's definition of the sales process differs markedly from those of his peers.

If polled, the average salesperson would probably define sales in more or less the same way, i.e., sales is the process by which he attempts to turn a suspect into a prospect and the prospect into a customer.

If asked, the Top Performer sees the sales process from a much broader perspective. He recognizes that his job begins long before he makes that initial contact with a suspect and that it continues long after the customer has crossed the last "T" of a contract.

The Top Performer sees himself as a manager over an entire process, not just the "Deal." He defines the sales process as one that encompasses all of the following components:

- Territory Planning – detailing how one can expect to meet revenue objectives.
- Territory Management – balancing time between prospecting or cold calling, closing, and moving prospects along in the selling cycle.
- Selling – defining the customer's business problems, developing a proposal in response to those problems,

identifying the key decision makers, overcoming objections, and finally, asking for and closing the sale.
• Servicing – maintaining existing accounts by meeting customer expectations.

2. The Top Performer has developed and utilizes several tools and techniques that enhance his chances of success.

3. The Top Performer is always open and receptive to new ideas that might improve his performance. In general, the difference between Average Performers and Top Performers during performance or sales call reviews is marked. Top Performers see these reviews as opportunities to learn. They ask questions until they understand their boss's perspective. They come into these reviews with an adult-to-adult attitude and make an effort to separate their egos from the professional goals they have set for themselves. Average Performers tend to become defensive and spend much of the time justifying why they did or did not do whatever is brought to their attention. This defensive attitude often renders them deaf to the very advice that, if taken, could transform them into Top Performers.

4. Top Performers tend to be driven. Many are driven by money. Others are driven by a desire to be recognized for what they are—"Top Performers." Still others are driven by an internal requirement to be the best they can be, to excel in their profession.

Of these characteristics, two can be taught. One can be trained to understand the sales process and trained to employ the tools and techniques that work. Openness and drive are another story and are harder to teach since they both must come from within. However, time and sensitive coaching can sometimes work to make people more receptive to the benefits of listening and learning.

The remainder of this book concentrates on the teachable components—the sales process and the tools and techniques used by Top Performers.

BASIC PRINCIPLES

Top Performers:

- Understand that success is dependent on one's ability to efficiently manage the sales process.

- Develop and utilize several tools and techniques that enhance the chances of success.

- Are always open and receptive to new ideas that might improve performance.

- Tend to be driven.

2

TERRITORY PLANNING

Like most salespeople, the Top Performer is action driven. The thought of sitting down and plotting out territory plans is just as tedious and distasteful to him as it is to you. He does not possess any magic formula that makes the task easier or more inviting. Territory planning is and always will be boring, monotonous, and time-consuming work.

All of us have a natural inclination to gravitate toward tasks that give us feelings of immediate accomplishment. Visiting a steady customer or preparing a sales presentation for a hot prospect are the kinds of things that give a salesperson a sense of satisfaction. It is easy for a salesperson to equate this kind of direct action with results. Plans, on the other hand, take time to prepare and to materialize. Planning cannot give that immediate sense of achievement, but the Top Performer forces himself to be forward thinking and disciplined. Like the prudent person who plans his retirement well in advance and the wise general who plans his battle strategy, the Top Performer recognizes the need to plan and map out his territory, even though he cannot see the immediate results.

The reward systems inherent in the business world do not make this an easy task. We are all programmed to think in terms of short-term results. It is a "make-the-month" attitude that, unfortunately, is reinforced so often by management. It takes real discipline not to succumb to this short-sighted mentality. The Top Performer has to work at it, knowing that his plans will not only keep him focused on the activities that will maximize his successes in the future, but will draw him back on course should he become distracted by day-to-day problems as well.

What will a good Territory Plan do?

A good territory plan serves several functions:

- It targets your market segments
- It defines your customer base within that market
- It identifies the customers from which you will attempt to get your revenue
- It details the specific actions required to close sales to those customers
- It recognizes the need for and develops different and specific plans for small, medium, and large companies within the targeted market segments.
- It provides a system for monitoring each activity.

The Territory Plan

A thorough territory plan consists of the following major components:

A. Sales Territory Overview
   1. Largest Cities
   2. Number of Companies by Market Segment
   3. Largest Companies
   4. Largest Existing Customers
   5. Major Competitive Accounts

B. Sales Forecast
   1. Forecast Assumptions
   2. Annual Forecast
   3. New Product Forecast

C. Revenue Stimulation Plans
 1. Goals and Objectives
 2. Strategies
 3. General Tactics/Programs
 4. Specific Tactics/Programs
 5. Customer Plans

D. Inhibitors for Meeting Revenue Objectives (Issues and Concerns).

There is no one best way to format your territory plan. Most companies have a set format that they prefer. The important thing to remember is that your plan should contain enough information to serve the functions previously listed, i.e., to target your market segments, define your customer base, etc.

The material needed for a territory plan may look like a lot of information to compile, but you need to remember that most of this information need only be gathered once and updated as required. All the information is important in order to develop an intelligent territory plan, and much of it can be obtained from local libraries.

A detailed sample territory plan can be found in the appendix.

Key Account Action Plans (KAAP)

In addition to a territory plan, the Top Performer develops detailed plans and strategies for his major accounts. In general, specific account plans should be developed for any customer that might be considered:

• A large revenue generator
• An account that may attract heavy competition
• Leading edge accounts in a major and/or new market segment, i.e., companies that are innovative and

creative and are watched and followed by other companies

A KAAP contains the following information:

A. Objectives
B. Organization Chart
C. Personnel Profiles
D. A definition of the customer's business problem
E. Competition
F. Sales Strategies and Action Plans
G. Issues and Concerns

A. Objectives

Objectives must be specific. To say, "Sell Company A $650,000 of product" is not specific enough. "Sell Company A $250,000 of Product X for application 1 and $400,000 of Product Z for application 2" is specific. Each product and application will require its own plan. In addition, the people involved, i.e., the key decision makers, may be different.

B. Organization Chart

An organization chart should be included in every KAAP. All key decision makers and influencers should be identified. Key decision makers are those who make the final decision, while the influencers may be defined as anyone to whom the key decision maker looks for recommendations. In many sales situations, the influencers are the key to the sale since their recommendations are usually heeded.

As Vice President of Sales and Marketing for Teletype, I approved the purchases for my organization. Therefore, I was the key decision maker. My department heads usually made their recommendations as to which products or services we should purchase. They were my influencers. I usually accepted their recommendations.

With major systems selling, you may encounter several important decision influencers. In these sales situations, you may expect to find someone from the financial organization, the technical organization, as well as someone from the user organization involved in the process. Take time to consider all the possible influencers. Many a sale has been lost because the competition did a better job of identifying and wooing the decision makers and influencers.

C. Personnel Profiles for Decision Makers/Influencers

Each KAAP should contain the following information regarding the key decision makers and influencers:

- Name
- Title
- The names of their subordinates
- Their job functions
- Their perceived attitude toward your company or product (Obviously, a negative attitude would require that you take actions to move that individual to a neutral or positive position.)
- Personality traits
- Special interests

D. A Definition of the Customer's Business Problem

This section of a KAAP contains the following:
- A definition of the customer's problem
- Individual decision makers/influencers problems
- Individual decision makers/influencers 'HOT' buttons
- Product fit with stated customer and individuals' business problems

Many salespeople lose sales because they do not take the time to identify what problem the customer is trying to solve by purchasing the product. Only by identifying the problem can the Top Performer position his product as a solution. (This will be discussed in detail, in Chapter 8, "Problem Solving/Consultative Selling.")

Key decision makers and influencers do not always give equal weight to all the company's problems. In making a decision, they tend to consider the problems that are most pressing to their particular organizations first. It is necessary to understand how each decision maker/influencer ranks the overall problems in importance.

For example, in a case cited in Chapter 8 the president of a company stated his company's need for timely and accurate sales information about fashion merchandise from each store. My product enabled the company to obtain information on sales, by item number, from each store within twenty-four hours. The company could then compile this information in one central location and prepare daily fashion sales reports. This feature was the merchandise department's "hot button." (Any feature that provides your customer with a solution to a problem and, in the process, excites and motivates them to purchase your product would be considered a "hot button.")

However, in this case, the store operations people were looking for a product that would improve the speed of customer check-out and give them daily departmental sales totals on the premises. Their decision was driven by a solution to these two issues. Speed of check-out, while important, was not a "hot button." It solved one of their problems but did not excite them the way the ability to obtain departmental totals on demand did. Our ability to solve both departments' key problems clinched the sale.

The list below identifies the issues that characteristically drive various types of decision makers and influencers.

Financial people tend to look at:

- Low cost of ownership
- Return on investment
- Break-even analysis
- Initial cost

Users tend to focus on:

- The best problem solution
- Reliability/maintainability
- Increased efficiency/productivity
- Ability to do job better/faster/easier
- Versatility
- Ease in learning
- Delivery time

Technical people look at:

- The best match with specifications
- Most up-to-date/technical solution
- Reliability/maintenance
- Price/performance[8]

E. Competition

This section should contain:
- Competitor's product fit with company problem
- Competitor's product fit with individual's problems/ hot buttons

[8]Miller and Heiman, *Strategic Selling,* Warner Books, 1985, p. 164.

F. Sales Strategies/Action Plans

Most salespeople have trouble differentiating what is a goal, what is a strategy, and what is a tactic. Don't get hung up on this. Simply put, this section should contain what you want to achieve (goals and objectives), how you plan to do it (strategies), and what you plan to do (tactics).

For each sales objective, specific strategies and tactics must be developed. Strategies and tactics should include details regarding:

- Seminars for executives and middle management
- Product demonstrations
- Existing customer site visits
- Visits to top management

When I was with the Teletype Corporation, we competed for a sizable printer order from a major airline. Having conducted business with Teletype several years before I had joined them, the company perceived that we would be slow to respond with any modifications they might require. They also questioned our ability to meet their service requirements. Obviously, we had a problem and had to change those perceptions if we were to have any chance of winning the order.

The following details the sales strategy and tactics we developed to change that customer's perceptions:

Strategies:

1. Respond to any customer requests within a two week period and attempt to make those responses positive.
2. Begin to build a bond between their top management and ours. (Most of our management at that time was new and had not met the customer's top management.)

3. Arrange a customer corporate visit to Teletype to demonstrate that we can support their future product and service requirements by:
   - Reviewing our technical support and service capability.
   - Detailing the new service procedure specifically designed to meet the customer's service requirements.
   - Sharing our future product plans to demonstrate that we can become a long-term provider of our product.

Tactics for Strategy 1:

1. Within fifteen days, set up a meeting with all Teletype vice presidents to review the account and stress the need for timely responsiveness to any request for product modifications and/or information.
2. Set up a subsequent meeting with those who report to the vice presidents to reiterate the same and carry the message to the "troops." Vice presidents will attend to reinforce the importance of the meeting.

Tactics for Strategy 2 & 3:

1. By July 1st, extend an invitation to the two key vice presidents at Arrow Air to visit Teletype. Our target date for the visit will be between August 1st - 15th. The invitation should be extended by our president. Have a letter outlining the agenda for the meeting ready for our president's review by July 15th.
2. Review the information to be presented by the Product and Service Managers by June 30th, including the new service procedure which will allow Arrow Air to:
   - Call one central dispatch number twenty-four hours a day.

- Have central dispatch call the service organization that is closest to the problem location.
- Provide monthly reports showing the problems and response times.
3. Dry run all the presentations by July 15th.

G. *Issues and Concerns*

Issues and Concerns in this section of your plan are any items that might negatively impact the account. For example:

"We have missed our last two commitments to deliver Product B to Mason & Dixon. If we do not deliver this product by January 15th, Mason & Dixon will, in all likelihood, purchase an equivalent product from our major competitor, resulting in a loss of all business from this account for the next year."

Sharing Your Plans With Your Customers

Now that you've invested all this time and effort developing your account plan for the upcoming year and have identified the business problems and applications on which you will be focusing, why not share your planned activities with your customers? You may consider this idea unusual, but it is the most sensible way to ensure that your plans are, indeed, the areas where your customers think emphasis is needed. The goals and objectives then become a team effort, i.e., your goals and your customer's become one and the same.

These account review meetings should be held with the customer's upper management either annually or semi-annually. They not only give you the chance to confirm and validate your upcoming plans, but they also provide you with an opportunity to review what you have done in the recent past in terms of service.

Most upper management personnel are not cognizant of what you have done to meet the needs of their people. Unfortunately, if anything, they are more likely to be brought in on the negative aspects of their associations with your company, i.e., a late delivery, a short shipment, etc. Rarely are they kept abreast of the things you may have done that might be considered "over and above" the call of duty. A review of your plans for the next six months or year gives you the chance to mention everything you've done for them. The review also serves to reinforce that you and your company are their problem solvers. Most companies are very receptive to this kind of review.

BASIC PRINCIPLES

A good territory plan:

• Has specific detailed account plans for each key account and defines what is going to be done, by whom and when.

• Recognizes the role of key decision makers and influencers and includes plans to address their chief concerns.

• Defines the customer's major business problems/ hot buttons.

• Addresses the needs of small and medium-sized customers.

• Has specific plans in place for the introduction of new products.

3

TERRITORY MANAGEMENT:
SALES IS A NUMBERS GAME

"Calls are the guts of this business."
Shelby H. Carter
Xerox Corporation

A number of years ago, I was appointed General Manager of a start-up division of General Instrument. The company manufactured a mini-computer-based payments processing system. The average sales price of the system was $200,000 with a selling cycle of approximately nine months. As a start-up, the division had a five person sales staff but no sales.

As was my habit, I spent my first few weeks conducting territory reviews and observing the existing patterns and techniques of my sales organization. It was not uncommon for my Midwestern salesperson to fly into Chicago for a meeting on Monday, then fly to Dallas for a single sales call on Tuesday, returning to New York Tuesday evening. Wednesday might be spent in the office, but he would be back on a plane by Thursday heading for, yet another, single sales call. The pace was grueling and hectic.

It wasn't long before I realized that this frantic pace was the predominant pattern for the entire sales organization. They crisscrossed the country in an effort to seize any sales opportunities that arose. Consequently, they spent much of their time in airports and on planes. They were working hard, but were they effective? It soon became clear that their haphazard travel schedules were such that they averaged only twelve face-to-face visits a month.

A different pattern became apparent when I was later appointed Vice President of Sales and Marketing for Teletype Corporation, a 400 million dollar subsidiary of AT&T. Teletype produced computer terminals, teleprinters, and computer printers that were sold primarily to the telephone operating companies and through original equipment manufacturers (O.E.Ms), and distributors. Once again, I conducted complete territory and account reviews prior to making any organizational changes. I also spent time with many of my salespeople reviewing their critical issues and concerns. It was during the course of these reviews that many of the account executives complained about their workloads. I conscientiously made note of their complaints and resolved to get to the bottom of them.

Over the next few weeks, I was surprised to learn that most of the sales organization never left the facility. I considered this quite puzzling in view of what so many of them had told me. If they weren't looking for business, what were they doing?

Each salesperson was traveling only four days a month, averaging eight face-to-face visits in that period. Clearly, this was unacceptable, but it certainly explained one of the reasons for the downward trend in the sales figures.

Still, it did not explain what the salespeople were doing with their time. Further investigation found that the salespeople were busy, but not necessarily with work that was directly related to acquiring new sales. Their time was being consumed with phone-in customer orders, answering technical questions, and handling customer complaints.

Organizational changes were obviously in order. I decided to divide my sales staff into inside and outside teams. The inside group became responsible for handling customer service calls, complaints, phone-in orders, and telemarketing, while the outside team was free to pursue sales. We began to see an improvement in the sales figures after a four month period.

I mention these two very different cases to emphasize one point. All too often salespeople forget that "sales is a numbers game." There is a direct correlation between the number of face-to-face customer contacts one schedules and the number of sales that are made.

Let's examine exactly how the number of sales calls impacts your revenue. The chart below will aid in this demonstration as well as in determining the number of cold calls you will need to make in order to meet your present revenue commitments.

1. Number of Closes per month.   _____
2. Ratio: Prospects/Closes   _____
3. Number of Prospects per month (1x2)   _____
4. Ratio: Suspects/Prospects   _____
5. Number of Suspects (3x4)   _____
6. Ratio: Number of Suspects/Cold Calls   _____
7. Number of Cold Calls per/mo. (5x6)   _____

For example, let us assume that your target is to close one new account per month. To achieve this you ordinarily call on two suspects before you get a true prospect. A suspect is an unqualified customer who has expressed an interest in your product. Usually a suspect is dropped after the second visit if no interest is apparent. A prospect is anyone who appears to have a need for your product or service. Further, with a prospect there is a strong possibility that a purchase will be made, either from you or a competitor. On average, for every four of your prospects, one will purchase. Another way to look at this is that 25 percent of your prospects will become actual customers.

Let's further assume that every five cold calls results in an appointment, i.e., a face-to-face meeting with a suspect. A cold call can be one that is made over the telephone or one in which you drop in on a suspect without an appointment.

Given this information let's fill in our hypothetical chart.

1. Number of Closes per month.	1
2. Ratio: Prospects/Closes	4
3. Number of Prospects per month (1x2)	4
4. Ratio: Suspects/Prospects	2
5. Number of Suspects (3x4).	8
6. Ratio: Number of Suspects/Cold Calls	5
7. Number of Cold Calls per/mo. (5x6)	40

In this example, forty cold calls are needed in order to close one new customer per month.

If that sounds overwhelming, remember that this only requires you to make two additional cold calls per day. *You could increase your closes by one per month, if you manage only two more face-to-face visits a week* (number of Suspects divided by 4 weeks).

Top Performers consistently make more sales calls than their peers. Top Performers understand that:

THE MORE FACE-TO-FACE VISITS YOU MAKE, THE MORE SALES YOU MAKE. THE MORE SALES YOU MAKE, THE MORE COMMISSIONS YOU EARN!

The individual that taught me the most about territory coverage and the importance of maximizing the number of face-to-face visits was Shelly K.

A typical day with Shelly began with a breakfast meeting at 7:30 A.M. His second sales call would be scheduled for

9:30 A.M. Depending on the anticipated length of that call, he usually attempted to fit in another sales call before lunch. Two or three calls in the afternoon were usual, followed by dinner with a customer.

Top Performers like Shelly averaged six to seven face-to-face visits a day, as compared to the Average Performer who might consider three to four calls a banner day. In two days, Shelly made as many calls as the Average Performer does in four days.

Obviously, the number of calls made per day will vary by industry and territory. For someone selling encyclopedias door-to-door, seven visits a day would be considered way below the industry norm. And it would be expected that someone covering a few-block area in a major city would be able to make many more calls than the salesperson who covers an entire city or region.

It would not be reasonable to expect Shelly to maintain that kind of pace on a daily basis. A major presentation to a customer might consume his entire morning. But what Shelly did was to maximize his "on-the-road" time. He carefully mapped out his trips and, in the process, had an average of two full days a week more than the Average Performer to use for proposals, office matters, phone follow-up, or for additional sales visits. As a Top Performer, Shelly clearly understood that his personal success depended, in part, on his adherence to a schedule that optimized his number of face-to-face visits.

BASIC PRINCIPLES

The more face-to-face visits you make, the more sales you make. The more sales you make, the more commissions you earn.

4

TERRITORY MANAGEMENT: THE FEAST OR FAMINE SYNDROME

Alex is flying high! He's Datatron's Golden Boy, having closed $160,000 worth of business. His boss is smiling a lot these days, and Alex, well, he's eyeing a new car. Of course, his wife might have something to say about what he's eyeing. She's been pouring over fabric and wallpaper books ever since he told her about the deal he closed at the beginning of this week. What the heck. He'll let her go to town in the living room and buy himself the car.

"Hey! I heard you closed the Phoenix deal!" Bill, the personnel director, says as he trots past Alex's door.

"Yeh! I sure busted my buns on that one. We got the go-ahead Monday!"

"Alright!" Bill clasps his hand in congratulations. "It's been a banner month for you, hasn't it?"

"It sure has!"

Bill starts back toward the door. "So what ya gonna do for an encore, Al? Sell a half-mil this month?"

Alex looks up. Bill is grinning like a Cheshire cat.

"Sure! Why not?" He grins right back, but the grin fades as soon as Bill is out of sight.

"What ya gonna do for an encore?"

Bill's words sink in hard and fast. Alex's stomach twinges just a bit.

"What am I going to do for an encore?"

23

Alex's stomach should be churning. A look at his schedule for the next month makes it turn right over. Alex has a problem. He's been working so hard to bring the three deals he just closed to the signing table that he's been neglecting his prospecting. Nothing is close to closing for at least three months, and his list of suspects is a little on the short side.

Golden Boy Alex is about to take a fall, and he only now realizes it. He's about to become a victim of the oldest sales malady in the book, "The Feast or Famine Syndrome." You all know the symptoms. The salesperson sees a couple of deals close to closing and he homes in on them, hungry for the taste of victory. He forgets about anything but the close. His cold calling falls by the wayside. Good suspects are put aside in favor of a visit to the "hot prospect that's close." Then, WHAMMO! The closes are reality and the salesperson is left with nothing but a nagging uneasiness about the future.

At this point most salespeople begin a frenzy of activity, in the hope of developing prospects overnight. But the odds for success are slim.

The Selling Cycle and its Contribution to the Syndrome

The selling cycle, that is the length of time between the initial customer contact and the placing of an order, can be quite lengthy in the systems-selling world. If your selling cycle is six months, in all likelihood it is going to take that full six months to turn any suspects you contact today into ordering customers.

Given that lengthy period, the systems salesperson is even more vulnerable than most to the "Feast or Famine Syndrome." For him, catching the syndrome could be deadly. And once he's got it there is no quick cure.

Veteran salespeople and Top Performers realize that the only way to prevent a recurrence is to maintain a steady, balanced diet of suspects, prospects, and customers. They force themselves to maintain schedules that give equal time to closing orders, prospecting and cold calling, and moving prospects along in the selling process.

BASIC PRINCIPLES

To avoid the "Feast or Famine Syndrome," you must balance your time between suspects, prospects, and customers.

5

TERRITORY MANAGEMENT: TOOLS AND TECHNIQUES TO MAXIMIZE CUSTOMER VISITS

In Chapter 3, we saw how critical the number of face-to-face visits was to sales success. In this chapter, we will take that same concept, go one step further, and deal with specific tools and techniques used by Top Performers to maximize that all-important "on-the-road" time.

Setting Up Your Sales Calls

You may have already marveled at Shelly's ability to squeeze the most out of his days. How did he do it? What techniques did he employ? How did he manage to set up his calls so efficiently? Let's look at the way the Average Performer (AP) schedules his visits and compare it to the way Shelly, a Top Performer (TP) would.

The Average Performer (AP) arrives at his office on Monday morning and scans his schedule for the week. He notes that he has no calls scheduled for Wednesday and Friday and none for three days the following week. He begins to make telephone calls.

> Secretary: Good morning. Mr. Jones's office. May I help you?
> AP: Good morning. This is AP. Is Mr. Jones in?

> Secretary: Yes, he is, but he's in a meeting at the moment. May I help you?
>
> AP: Do you know how long he will be?
>
> Secretary: He's in his Monday morning staff meeting. It's hard to tell.
>
> AP: I would like to get together with him either this week or next. Would you please have him call me back when he's free? I'll be here all day. My number is . . .

Later

> AP: Hello, this is Average Performer.
>
> Jones: Hello, AP, this is Harold Jones.
>
> AP: Hi, Harold. I'm happy you returned my call. You raised a number of questions on the proposal I gave you. I have all the answers for you and would like to meet with you this week, if at all possible.
>
> Jones: Sorry, AP, but this week is out.
>
> AP: How about next week?
>
> Jones: Gee! Next week looks bad too. How about the following week?
>
> AP: (I had planned to go to Boston that week. What lousy luck! I have plenty of time this week and next week.) Okay, how about Monday of that week?
>
> Jones: That's fine. How does nine o'clock sound to you?
>
> AP: See you then.

The Top Performer (TP) comes in on Monday, peruses his calendar and sees that his next two weeks are booked. He begins to plan which part of his territory he will visit three and four weeks out and isolates which customers/prospects he plans to visit. He decides to visit Boston in three weeks and Washington, D.C., in four weeks. He selects the two or three major prospects/customers he feels he must see and begins making telephone calls.

> Secretary: Good morning. Ms. Boyd's office. May I help you?
>
> TP: Good morning, Betty. This is TP. How are you today?

Secretary: I'm fine, and yourself?

TP: Very well, thank you. How are your wedding plans progressing?

Secretary: I can't believe you'd remember! Everything is moving according to schedule. We've picked a place for the wedding and made some tentative honeymoon plans.

TP: That's great! Where are you going?

Secretary: To Hawaii, can you believe it?

TP: Sounds perfect. My wife and I have been to Hawaii. Remind me to tell you about it when I see you . . . which leads me to the reason I've called. I plan to be in Boston in three weeks and I'd like to set up an appointment to see Rita. Is she there?

Secretary: She is, but she's at her Monday morning staff meeting.

TP (Realizing that Rita may not be available for several hours) How does her schedule look for the morning of August 16th?

Secretary: Let me see now . . . her schedule looks pretty clear. Should I have her call you?

TP: I'd like to meet with Rita for about an hour at 9:00 A.M. on August 16th. Would you call me back and let me know if this time is convenient for her? If I'm not here, perhaps you can leave a message with my secretary. If she can't see me then, would you please find out what times are convenient for her and leave that information?

Secretary: I'll talk to her as soon as she gets out of her meeting and get back to you.

TP: That'd be great. Thank you, Betty. See you in three weeks.

Let's now analyze the differences between the Average Performer and the Top Performer.

1. Mr. Jones, like many business people, had his calendar booked for the coming weeks. The Average Performer was locked out of that week and the next. AP is now left with several empty, unproductive days that might have been filled

had he planned his call a few weeks sooner. The Top Performer has learned that the further ahead he sets up his appointments, the easier and more likely it is that he will get the appointment he needs when he wants it.

THE TOP PERFORMER SETS UP TERRITORY VISITS AT LEAST THREE WEEKS IN ADVANCE.

2. The Top Performer avoids playing telephone tag by making effective use of the customer's secretary to set up the appointment. The Average Performer hasn't set up anything but a game of telephone tag that could last for days. He has even gone so far as to promise to make himself available for the remainder of the day in order to be there for the call back.

THE TOP PERFORMER MAKES EFFECTIVE USE OF SECRETARIES TO MAKE HIS APPOINT- MENTS.

3. Notice that the Top Performer has set a time limit for his meeting. Rita will appreciate that and will be far more likely to fit him in, if she knows how much of her time will be required.

THE TOP PERFORMER SETS TIME LIMITS FOR THE SAKE OF HIS SCHEDULE AS WELL AS FOR THOSE OF HIS CUSTOMERS.

4. Remember the regional salesperson I mentioned in Chapter 3, the one who crisscrossed the country in response to his customers' schedules? The Average Performer has set himself up in much the same way. The Top Performer is controlling who he sees and when he sees them by setting up his appointments three and four weeks in advance. He can plan several calls in the same area for the same day because he has scheduled appointments well in advance.

THE TOP PERFORMER LEARNS TO MAXIMIZE HIS PRODUCTIVITY AND, THEREFORE, HIS REVENUE.

When I review these basics of territory management with salespeople, they always give reasons why they fail to set up their appointments three and four weeks in advance. Let's take a moment to explore the most common reason given: "I've got to keep my calendar clear. I've got a deal about to close."

I have seen days pass into weeks waiting for the BIG call, while promising opportunities slip away. I tell the salespeople who have worked for me, "Forget about leaving time on your calendars waiting for the BIG call. If and when that call comes in, you will be able to work it into your existing schedule or, if you have to, you will make arrangements to reschedule some of your other appointments."

Using The Secretary To Set Up Appointments

When you ask salespeople why they chose sales as their profession, one of the most common reasons given is that they like people. Yet, they often spend very little time getting to know or learn about the people with whom they do business.

The Top Performer is a people person too, but he takes the time to find out about people. He does not limit himself to the people with whom he will eventually negotiate a sale, but is just as interested in getting to know the "nuts and bolts" people as he is the vice presidents and presidents. He is careful to keep his conversations brief and professional, but also friendly.

The Top Performer knows that, contrary to popular belief, most people want to be helpful. Given an opportunity, most of the people he meets will want to help him once they get to know him personally.

Where the average salesperson hops from phone booth to phone booth, playing telephone tag with his customers, the Top Performer sees the customer's secretary as someone who, if given the opportunity, can and will help him to maximize his time by relaying messages and scheduling appointments. He makes a point of establishing a good working relationship with her.

"But come on, I usually only talk to a secretary over the phone for a few minutes and only see her when she escorts me into my customer's office. How can I be expected to establish a relationship with her in that short period of time?" you ask.

You should make the effort, and it can be done in the time you have. Let's examine how the Top Performer does it.

In many companies, the customer's secretary is sent to escort the salesperson to and from the customer's office. For the Top Performer, the few minutes it takes to walk down the hall provides an excellent opportunity to get to know the secretary.

Many of us find first conversations difficult. How does one begin? What does one say? The icebreakers for conversation can take any number of forms. While comments on the weather or the traffic or even the apparent busyness of the office may seem ridiculously mundane, they can quickly lead to more interesting topics if the salesperson is open and attentive.

The following conversation illustrates this point. Note how the Top Performer manages to start a simple, friendly conversation as he is escorted down the hall, then quickly makes it more engaging through thoughtful questioning.

TP: Is it always this muggy in Dallas?

Secretary: It's been this way for two weeks. The summers can be pretty brutal down here.

TP: Whew! I feel like I could wring out my suit. I take it you are used to it. Have you lived around here for some time?

Secretary: No, actually I'm from San Francisco. I've only been in Dallas about six months.

TP: San Francisco is one of my favorite cities, but how did you end up in Dallas?

Secretary: My husband got a job with Rockwell.

TP: What does he do for them?

Secretary: He's an electrical engineer. He was hired by Rockwell to work on new central office telephone equipment they are designing. (Arriving at Mr. Cramer's Office) Here we are. This is Mr. Cramer's office.

TP: Thank you, Pam.

Let's step back now and look at what the Top Performer found out about Pam in the few minutes he had before his meeting with Mr. Cramer.

Pam is from San Francisco.
She has been in the area about six months.
Her husband is an electrical engineer.
He works for Rockwell, designing central office equipment.

Top Performers are quick to pick up on the many clues around them. Listen for accents. Could the secretary have moved from another part of the country? If so, how did she arrive in her present position? How long has she lived in this community? Is the facility new? How long have they been in their present headquarters? Are their posters and pictures in and around the desk that could help you home in on other interests? Does Pam have a family? Do the pictures or posters indicate an interest in sports? A Top Performer knows that people like to talk about their families, hobbies, and interests.

In the event that Pam was not asked to escort him from his meeting, he would make a special point of stopping to say goodbye to her. A friendly, "try to stay cool," or "hope to see you again," or "it was nice meeting you," does much to cement the Top Performer's name and face with the very person who, in all likelihood, will screen his next call to the customer.

I have talked to several secretaries in the process of writing this book. All of them have told me that they remember the salespeople who show consideration and interest for them as people. Take the time to establish friendly relationships with secretaries and receptionists.

Do not misunderstand my intention in including this advice. It is not meant to encourage you to pursue conversations for the sole purpose of using the secretary's friendship in the future. It is included as a way of demonstrating how you can break the ice with people you encounter in your business life, people you have a sincere interest in drawing out and getting to know.

Insincerity can be sensed, and your interest then becomes intrusive prying. In that case, your questions will do more harm than good, since a perceptive person will then be anything but helpful to you.

In the case I have presented, the Top Performer is well on his way toward establishing a friendly relationship with Pam. In future conversations, he would try to find out even more about her. How did she feel about leaving San Francisco? How long did she live there? What does she like about California? What does she dislike? Does she like Texas?

In these subsequent visits and phone calls, the Top Performer would continue to share some of his own background with her as well. For the Top Performer, this is the enjoyable part of sales, meeting people and getting to know them.

Setting Time Limits

You may have noticed that the Top Performer sets a time limit for his meetings whenever possible. You should get into this routine as well. For one thing, it allows you to plan your schedule better. Meetings that are open-ended tend to drag, making it difficult to keep scheduled appointments. If a time limit has been set prior to the meeting, you will also find that you and your customer will use the allocated time better. In all likelihood, your customer will have scheduled another meeting following yours and will be mindful of the need to cover all the important items within the time that is allowed. The Top Performer has also learned that people appreciate it when you show consideration for their time.

Obviously, it is easier to schedule a short meeting. People are much more receptive to thirty-minute meetings than those that are an hour or more. You will be far more successful making appointments if you are mindful of this. However, if you have agreed to thirty minutes, do not go into the meeting expecting to stretch it out. That is highly inconsiderate and builds resentment.

I once set up a meeting with a vice president of AT&T and his staff to review data products my company was attempting to sell to them. I had requested an hour. At the end of the hour, we still had not been able to cover all the material I had anticipated we could.

"I guess I had not anticipated so many questions," I told the vice president. "However, I only asked for an hour of your time and I see that the hour is up. I have time, but I realize that you might have scheduled other appointments. If it is inconvenient to continue at this time, perhaps I could set up another appointment."

The vice president replied," I appreciate you holding to your scheduled time. I do have another appointment, but I believe that Tom and Dick can stay. Perhaps they can cover the open ground and report back to me."

If you have agreed to an hour, design your presentation or demonstration for approximately forty minutes, allowing time for questions. Always show respect for your customer's schedule.

Maximizing Unexpected Field Time

Now that the Top Performer has set up his key contacts for the coming weeks, he focuses his attention on other customers that he wants to visit in the surrounding areas. He immediately begins to set up other appointments.

Scheduling Around Key Visits

As a result of meeting cancellations or meetings that are completed faster than expected, there will be days when TP has unscheduled time on his hands.

TP sees this as an unexpected opportunity. He consults his customer list and decides to call Mark Perkes.

> Secretary: Good Morning. Mr. Perkes's office.
>
> TP (after spending a minute in conversation with the secretary): I just got into town. Last week we introduced a new splice that I know Mark would like to see. Is he available to see me for about thirty minutes at three today?
>
> or
>
> TP: I just got into town. I didn't schedule an appointment to see Mark this visit, but I received the information he requested just before I left the office. Would he be able to see me for a short meeting at three o'clock today?
>
> Secretary: He's at a meeting right now, Jonathan, and his schedule looks tight all day.
>
> TP: I realize it's short notice. Why don't I call you back in an hour? Perhaps some time will free up and he'll be able to see me. I believe he wanted to review the information I've obtained for him.

Top Performer may or may not be able to see Mr. Perkes that day, but he will continue to call on customers, prospects, or make cold calls right up to his next scheduled meeting. He never wastes time.

For example, Top Performer, who is based in California, has been unsuccessful in establishing who oversees the projects that require fiber optic products for a major company in Colorado. Having finished an appointment earlier than she had planned in Colorado, she decides to visit this company to see if she can determine which engineer is in charge of any ongoing projects that require fiber optic products.

At the visitor's entrance, she explains to the receptionist who she is trying to locate. Using the lobby phone and with the help of the receptionist, she is able to locate the correct person. The engineer cannot meet with TP on short notice, but does agree to meet with her at a future date.

In twenty minutes, TP has successfully accomplished what she had been unable to accomplish in several weeks of calls from the West Coast.

Some people believe that "dropping in" is a waste of time. I disagree. Around thirty percent of the people will meet with you on short notice, if the meeting is to be brief and they are interested in what you are selling. It has been my experience that if you take the time to drop off literature for a suspect or a prospect, he or she will be more receptive to seeing you the next time you call to set up an appointment.

Scheduling the Next Visit

TP has completed a meeting with Rita. Unlike the Average Performer, who might wait to reschedule the next meeting, TP consults his calendar prior to leaving her office. He sees that he plans to be in Boston again in three weeks.

> TP: Rita, why don't we plan to get together again in three weeks. I'm sure that by that time you'll probably have several other questions, and I should have answers for all the questions you raised today. How is either nine o'clock on September 13th or three o'clock that same day?

Rita: Nine o'clock looks good. I'll call you if any other
   questions come up.

TP: Great! That way I'll be prepared with answers to all your
   concerns. See you in three weeks.

Not only has TP saved himself the trouble of having to
place another call to Rita after he returned to his office, but
he has successfully controlled the tempo of the sale.

Cold Calling

These two words instill more dread and fear in the
hearts of salespeople than any others. Oh! How we hate it!
We will do almost anything to avoid having to make that
unsolicited call or visit. We'd sooner sit down to write that
boring territory plan than subject ourselves to one slamming
door, right?

This aversion is based on a fear of rejection and failure.
Of course, knowing that doesn't make cold calling any easier.
How many times have you caught yourself saying, "I wouldn't
mind doing this if the company gave me qualified leads." or
"We should hire telemarketing people to do this." This kind
of complaining is your anxiety speaking.

Cold calling is tough! Nothing I can tell you will ensure
that you will never hear the clunk of a dead phone in your ear
or guarantee that you will never see the grain on the back of
a customer's door. There aren't any magic formulas that will
ensure that you will always meet with success.

What I can give you are a few tips that will maximize
your chances of success and arm you with a quotation that I
use when the going gets rough.

Someone once asked Edison," How did you feel when
you had failed over one thousand times?"

"I didn't fail a thousand times," he responded. "I learned a thousand ways that it wouldn't work."

The only way to ensure that you will not fail is to do nothing. And remember, doing nothing renders nothing when payday arrives.

Finding Leads

The sources for leads vary from company to company and industry to industry. Most companies provide their salespeople with lead lists that they have compiled from ads, call-ins, direct mail responses, telemarketing, shows, etc. This list and the handy yellow pages are usually the primary sources for unqualified leads.

But did you know that most communities offer more detailed information about local businesses through their Chambers of Commerce? A simple phone call can provide you with a wealth of information about businesses in your territory. For example, the Denver Chamber of Commerce publishes a yearly membership directory that lists every major employer and Chamber member in the metropolitan region. It identifies the number of employees with each major company and the specific products they sell. Members are not only listed by company, but by job title as well. In addition, the Chambers provide information on local business networks and organizations (CEO Forums, Small Business Development Centers etc.) that may prove useful, and details regarding clubs and organizations that are industry- or interest-specific.

A local library can also be an excellent source of information. Reference librarians can direct you to lists of companies by area, revenue, industry (listed by SIC codes—Standard Industry Classification codes), number of employees, and any number of categories that you might not have known existed.

Often, your customers can be your best source of leads. After you have successfully closed and installed your product or service, do you routinely ask your customer if he can think of anyone else who might be in the market for your product? Probably not. But what could be easier than asking? If you have serviced him well, he will be more than happy to refer you to other business acquaintances who might be in need of your product or services. He might even be willing to call the referrals and to introduce you personally. At the very least, ask him if you can use his name as a reference in the future.

Telephone Cold Calling

Whenever you cold call by phone, you usually have two goals. The first goal is to qualify the suspect or prospect. The second goal is to set up a visit for a qualified prospect. However, there are times when you cannot adequately qualify a suspect over the phone. In general, the more complex the sale, the more difficult it is to qualify over the phone. There is just too much information that has to be gathered in order to determine if the product is suitable to the suspect's needs. This is especially true with systems selling. In these cases, a face-to-face visit is necessary just for qualification purposes.

Many times a suspect may tell you that he or she has no need for your product, but after a visit you are able to determine if he or she may have a need in the future. In these cases, the opportunity to meet the customer face-to-face and maintain contact will put you in an excellent position when the customer is ready to buy.

Goal Setting

Cold calling discipline is essential. No matter how loathsome you find it, you must set a goal for yourself. Many salespeople set a time goal; "I will call for two hours." I prefer a goal that focuses on results, not time; "I will call until I have set up four appointments." But whatever goal you choose to set, devote at least a little of each day to cold calling. That approach is kinder to the psyche than devoting one entire day.

Ask your secretary to hold all calls, and emphasize that you would prefer no interruptions. I have found that most salespeople look for any reason to avoid cold calling and thus see interruptions as welcome excuses.

Another popular technique used by many Top Performers is to keep a log in order to see and measure improvement. We seldom see our progress in this area unless it is written out and placed in front of us. At the very minimum, the log should contain the number of calls made per hour and the number of appointments that are set up.

Getting a Prospect's Attention

The key to telephone prospecting is to get the prospect's attention in the first ninety seconds. Remember that the prospect is not interested in what you are selling, but only in what the product will do for his/her company. In order to get the prospect's attention, you must focus on the advantages that your product can bring to his business.

For example, a company I once assisted sold a credential search service to hospitals and doctors. Among the problems the company faced were that many hospitals used their own staff members to check the credentials of potential employees. For a fee this company did a much more thorough job and were often much more successful in ferreting out potential employees who had been dismissed because of poor job performance. They also took the time to validate any schooling or degrees that were mentioned on résumés. Unfortunately, because they charged a fee for a service that was usually performed at no cost by staff members, it was difficult to get hospitals and doctors to listen. A typical conversation with a hospital administrator often went like this:

> Jodi O.: Hello. This is Jodi O. I am with Hospital Credentials. Our company does credential checks for new doctor hires. I would like an opportunity to meet with you to explain our service.
> Hospital Administrator: We do credential checks ourselves and have no need for outside assistance.

At this point, Jodi O. had, in all likelihood, already lost the prospect. However, after working with the company, modifications were made in the initial contact approach.

> Jodi O.: Hello, my name is Jodi O. and I am with Hospital Credentials. Many hospitals are seeing an increase in insurance costs because of the number of malpractice suits being brought to court. I assume that you and General Hospital are also concerned about this growing trend.
> Hospital Administrator: We are.
> Jodi O.: Our research has found that one of the reasons for this disturbing trend is because so many hospitals are hiring doctors unaware that the doctors do not meet their hospital's standards. Normal reference checks don't always unearth cases where doctors have been given the option to leave in lieu of the hospital taking disciplinary action against them. I don't know if you've had that kind of problem, but can you see how poor reference checking can put your hospital at risk?
> Hospital Administrator: I can.
> Jodi O.: My company specializes in the area of medical reference checking. I would like to take thirty minutes of your time to share with you how you can reduce the threat of malpractice suits and the subsequent increases in insurance premiums by using our service.

Using this approach, Jodi prequalifies the customer and establishes that the hospital personnel agrees that the problem she describes exists. If the customer balked at a visit, she would ask, "Isn't thirty minutes a small investment of your time when you consider the fact that our service could provide real safeguards against the possibility of costly lawsuits?"

Given ninety seconds to get someone's attention, you will only be successful if you can position the benefits your service or product can bring to the customer. If they do not agree that they have a problem, you will never have a sale! Don't waste time with idle information. Focus on the customer's business problem and work to reach an agreement.

Let's look at yet another case:

Shari P.: Hello, my name is Shari P. I'm with Record Management Consulting Services. We specialize in the design of record management systems with specific emphasis on filing, storage, retention and microfilming systems. I would like to set up a meeting with you to show you what we can do for your company.

Using this approach, Shari had difficulty setting up appointments. By modifying her presentation to focus on the benefits of her services to the customer, she significantly improved the ratio of appointments to calls.

Shari P.: Hello, my name is Shari P. I'm with Record Management Consulting Services. My company designs record and information systems, an area most companies overlook when they are looking to save money. Has your company ever considered looking into this area to reduce costs?

Prospect: No, we haven't.

Shari P.: The best way to demonstrate what is possible is to review what we've done for some of our clients. One of our customers not only saved $100,000 in the first year after we installed a new record retention system, but saw significant improvements in the ability to access their records. For another, we revised their filing system and eliminated the need for two clerks. A third saw a reduction of 40 percent in the cost of microfilming production. If you could give me thirty minutes of your time, I could explain our service and the possibilities it might have for you and your company."

How many people would say no to these approaches? If the potential customer is still hesitant, it is often helpful to ask him to explain why he does not feel the need to give you some of his time. Very often, his very explanation can present opportunities to demonstrate how your product could help him.

BASIC PRINCIPLES

Setting Up Face-To-Face Visits

- Set up visits at least three weeks in advance.
- Set time limits for your meeting.
- Use the secretary to set up visits.
- Try to set up the next meeting when you are there.

Cold Calling

- You have ninety seconds to get your customer's attention.
- Try to reach agreement on the problem.
- Focus on the benefits your product can bring to the customer.

6

SELLING:
STEPS OF THE SALES CALL

Kathy and I were following up on an inquiry from a distributor who had expressed interest in handling our fiber optic product line. Following introductions, Kathy began:

> Kathy: We are following up on your telephone inquiry. We understand that you are interested in receiving some information about being a distributor for our products.
>
> Customer: Yes, we are interested in getting into fiber optic products.
>
> Kathy: That fits in perfectly with our plans as well. At present, we do not have a distributor covering this area. Let me begin by telling you about our company and our product line.
>
> M.L.: Before you do that, perhaps Bob could tell us a little about his company. (Turning to the customer) Unfortunately, I am not as familiar with it as Kathy is.

(Before the visit, I had taken some time to find out about this distributor. However, because they were a privately owned company, the information I could obtain was very general. They enjoyed a good reputation in the area and appeared to be the kind of company that we would be interested in signing to handle our products.)

> Customer: The company was started in 1982 by John Williams, our president, and his brother, Peter, who heads up the purchasing department. Today, we employ forty people.

We have five outside salespeople and twenty customer service reps who take orders and do telemarketing. Our primary market is equipment manufacturers, but we also sell to the telephone market on occasion.

M.L.: You've seen some nice growth in the company. John Williams must be proud of what he has accomplished.

Customer: Oh! Yes, he is.

M.L.: To what do you attribute the company's success?

Customer: John and Pete have built the company on quality products and on-time delivery. We take a special pride that our delivery record is one of the best in the business. We deliver a product on the committed date.

(The customer had given me the company's "hot buttons." Bob told me that the company was built on quality products and on-time delivery. Naturally, these two criteria would be important considerations to them in selecting a manufacturer to supply them with fiber optic products. Kathy and I would want to stress our company's adherence to these same standards when we stated why we thought they should distribute our products. In her hurry to plug our product line, Kathy had missed an important opportunity to determine the criteria this company had for vendor selection.)

M.L.: That's very interesting because, as you review our company, I believe that you will find that it was also built on pride in our quality and our good delivery record. How do you train your people?

Customer: That is a very important point. We won't take on any line unless our people are provided with adequate training.

(Again, another "hot button" had been established. In this situation, there was an excellent match between the customer and my company. But never tell a customer something because it's what he or she wants to hear. This strategy invariably backfires. Honesty is not only the best policy, it should be your only policy.)

M.L.: Good! That fits in with our philosophy as well. We will not give our line to a distributor who will not allow us to train his people. Experience has shown us that without proper training, you will not be successful. Also, it costs you money when customers are given the wrong information or sold the wrong product.

Later, in our presentation, Kathy and I emphasized the capabilities that most closely matched the customer's criteria for vendor selection. After our presentation, the customer excused himself. When he came back, he told us that he would like us to meet with his president for about ten minutes. Thirty minutes later, we left the president's office with an understanding that his company would carry our product.

Kathy was an outstanding professional salesperson but in this situation she forgot the basics of selling. Her ultimate objectives were the same as mine, but in her eagerness, Kathy had skipped the first critical step of a sales call.

Your understanding and execution of all the steps in a sales call, as well as the proper allocation of your time to each step, will play an important part in determining how successful you will be.

Steps Of A Sales Call

1. Fact Gathering

A basic knowledge of the customer's business and company is critical to a sale. Gather as much information as possible regarding the customer's business problems, the company's organizational structure, its approval cycles, and establish who the decision makers and influencers are early on. While not all sales require the formulation of a KAAP (Key Account Action Plan), all the customer information contained in such a plan must be obtained, regardless of the size of the company.

As part of the fact-gathering process, Top Performers realize that it is important to determine quickly if the sales opportunity is real. It amazes me how many seasoned professionals fail to qualify their prospects. A Top Performer knows that he cannot afford to waste time with nonbuyers or spend an inordinate amount of time with those who are not in a decision making or influencing position.

2. *Position your product to solve the customer's business problem*

It is important to note that while the Average Performer sell products, the Top Performer sells solutions to problems. A Top Performer takes the time to understand the customer's business problem so that he can effectively show how his product will solve that problem.

3. *Handling Objections*

Most salespeople are uncomfortable hearing objections. They try to avoid situations that might lead to the raising of objections. But the Top Performer goes out of his way to solicit any customer concerns, realizing that it is easier to sell to a buyer who expresses an objection than one who has concerns he keeps to himself. When the buyer states an objection, it gives the Top Performer an opportunity to respond and satisfactorily address the customer's concerns.

4. *Closing*

Personally, I believe there has been too much emphasis on this one step, to the detriment of other steps of the sales process. Seeking concurrence from the customer throughout each step of the sales process makes closing an evolutionary, rather than a revolutionary process.

Time Allocations

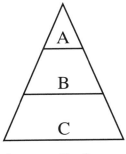

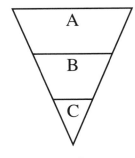

Average Performer   Top Performer

In both of these diagrams, "A" represents the fact-finding/gathering part of the selling process. "B" represents the amount of time that should be devoted to moving the customer along in the selling process, and "C" represents the time that should be given over to closing. Surprised?

The Average Performer is forced to spend an inordinate amount of time asking for and pursuing an order, that is, trying to close. He has a chronic difficulty with closing because he does not spend enough time working in steps A and B. It is in step A that he should determine his customer's business problems, identify the key decision makers, and uncover his customer's "hot buttons." These discoveries are then used as the foundation for his sales strategies, proposals, and presentations. Unfortunately, without the time invest-ment in steps A and B, the Average Performer is unable to address his or her customer's concerns satisfactorily. Hence, the Average Performer is forced to spend most of his time trying to close an order.

Kathy skipped the fact-gathering stage of selling. She was so eager to discuss her product that she missed the chance to discover the three key "hot buttons" that eventually became the focus of our successful sales presentation. Kathy would have probably uncovered these "hot buttons" at some point, but our first and only presentation was much more effective because we had spent those few minutes gathering important information from the customer. The customer's concerns with quality, on-time delivery, and training, uncovered before any discussion of our product, allowed us to present our company's record in this area and get an immediate commitment from the president.

BASIC PRINCIPLES

The four steps in a sales call are:

• Fact Gathering

• Positioning your product to solve the customer's business problem

• Handling objections

• Closing

Average Performers characteristically have trouble closing because they do not spend enough time in the first three steps of the selling process.

7

SELLING:
FACT GATHERING

Let's look at how the Average Performer and Top Performer approach a new prospect.

> AP: Good morning, John. It's nice to meet you. I'm AP.
> John: Nice to meet you, AP.
> AP: We received your inquiry on our terminal equipment. I appreciate you giving me the opportunity to review our products.
> John: We are looking to buy about one hundred terminals and thought it would be important to look at what your company and product have to offer us.
> AP: Let me review our product line and answer any questions you might have.

The Top Performer handles his first conversation with John quite differently.

> TP: Good morning, John. It's nice to meet you. I'm TP.
> John: Nice to meet you, TP.

TP wants to put both his prospect and himself at ease. Knowing that people like to talk about themselves, he opens the conversation with a question relating to John. He looks around the office and notices a diploma hanging on the wall. John had received a B.M.E. degree.

TP: I noticed that your degree is in mechanical engineering. How did you make the transition to Data Processing?
John: When I left school . . .

John proceeds to tell TP about his transition to Data Processing and his business career. As John talks, TP asks him additional questions in order to learn more about him.

TP: That's quite a story. My background isn't anywhere near as interesting. I started off in . . .

By sharing a little of his own background, TP has begun to establish a rapport with the customer. He will build on that in future visits.

TP: John, I'm not as familiar with your company as I would like to be. Perhaps you can give me some background information on your company and its products.

At this point, John would update TP on his company and its products. As they talk, TP would ask additional questions to improve his understanding of the company's needs and focus.

TP: I appreciate the information. Before going into the specific details about my company and our products, perhaps you could give me a brief overview of your organization and tell me why you are interested in our products.

Let's examine the techniques used by Top Performer that will contribute to his success.

The Icebreaker

The Top Performer does not begin his presentation until he has spent some time learning about the customer as a person. In order to do this, the Top Performer must be observant. As he did with the secretary in an earlier chapter, he seeks out personal items such as diplomas, family pictures, sport trophies or other objects in the customer's office that might help him begin a conversation.

In the previous example, the Top Performer noticed the diploma on John's wall, which helped him initiate the conversation. He also might have chosen to make the subjects of a family portrait his conversation opener. In situations where no personal items are obvious, the Top Performer might begin by inquiring about how long John had been with the company or how long he had lived in that part of the country.

Fact Gathering

The Top Performer does his homework and knows about the company and its products, but in order to be successful he realizes that he must know more than this basic information. Asking the customer nonthreatening questions about his company accomplishes two things. First, it relaxes the customer by giving him something to talk about that he knows well, and second, it gives Top Performer interesting insights into the company that might prove helpful later in the selling process. Another way to obtain the answers you need is to ask for an organization chart. This is especially important when dealing with large organizations.

> "Perhaps I could obtain an organization chart? I find this really helpful when dealing with large companies. It helps me understand the respective roles of the individuals I am dealing with."

In my experience, no one has ever refused to give me or draw an organization chart. As you review the chart, don't forget to ask questions. During this fact-gathering period, ask different questions to crosscheck your understanding of who the key decision makers and influencers in the company are.

"As I understand it, these will be the people involved in the final decision."

This will ensure that there will be no surprises as you move through the selling cycle. It is helpful to ask different people within the organization the same questions. You'd be surprised how many times you will get different answers.

It is also surprising the number of times you will discover other people who will become involved in the purchasing decision. Reconfirm what you are told. You don't want to get blind-sided.

Don't wear out your welcome. The fact-gathering stage usually encompasses several visits. Don't ask too many questions in your initial visit. As you spend more time with the customer and get to know him, you will be able to gain more insights into your account.

Develop a Rapport with the Customer

Top Performers know that people like to do business with people they know. Another advantage of beginning with personal questions and sharing some of your background is that it begins the process of establishing a rapport with your customer. The best way to get to know someone is out of the office, over lunch or dinner. I see this as an opportunity to get to know the people I work with and vice versa, not as an opportunity to try and sell my prospect. In these situations, keep the sales pitch to a minimum and the conversation light, unless you have agreed with your customer that the primary purpose of the meal is to conduct business.

Determining If the Opportunity is Real

Jim C. and I were visiting one of Jim's hot prospects, a bank that was interested in our payment processing system. On Jim's last forecast, he had indicated that he expected to close this business within thirty days. The visit was going very well, and it was obvious that the customer was very enthusiastic about our equipment. I waited for Jim to ask the significant question, "When can we expect to receive a purchase order?"

When Jim didn't ask, I asked.

> M.L.: From the conversation, I assume you are excited about our equipment and will be placing an order?
> Customer: That's correct!
> M.L.: What is the next step? Is there anything we can do to expedite the order?
> Customer: The next step is that I have to complete my recommendation to my boss, who is the VP of Finance.
> M.L.: When do you anticipate completing this?
> Customer: Given my present workload, I should have that done within three weeks.
> M.L.: What happens after that?
> Customer: Since the expenditure is for $250,000, it must go to the capital appropriations committee and then, on to the Board of Directors.
> M.L.: How long does that usually take?
> Customer: If there are no major issues or questions raised, the process usually takes three months. Unfortunately, if they are backed up with any other expenditures, it could take up to six months.

Carried away by his customer's enthusiasm, Jim had never bothered to find out about the lengthy approval cycle. He did eventually get the order, but it certainly wasn't within the time frame that he had predicted in his forecast. The order didn't come through for another six months.

How could Jim have avoided this? How can you tactfully find out if the opportunity is real and imminent?

The Average Performer assumes that any interest in his product is a buying situation. The Top Performer knows that is not the case. He has learned that the only way to find out if an opportunity is there is to ASK!

The Average Performer is reluctant to ask questions. I have never been able to determine if this reluctance is because he is afraid to rock the boat, thinking that such questions might appear intrusive and pushy, or if he is insecure and fears the possible objections that his customer might raise.

People are generally quite willing to respond to nonthreatening questions. Top Performers know that and ask a lot of questions until they are sure that they have all the facts. Top Performers ask the same questions in different ways to assure themselves that they have not misunderstood what the customer has told them.

Below are several of the typical questions that Top Performers might pose when they need to determine if the sales opportunity is real or want to assess the length of their customers' approval cycles.

To determine whether the company is buying or just gathering information:

"What is your time frame for making this decision?
"Has this purchase already been budgeted?"

If the customer has no specific time frame or informs you that he is at the information gathering point, you might want to follow up with:

"What happens with the information that you gather?"
"What determines whether you go any further with this?"
"What factors will encourage your company to look at purchasing this equipment?"

To determine the length and kind of approval cycle you may expect:

"What is the decision-making process at ABC Computer?"

"Who gets involved in the purchase decision?"
"How long does the decision process usually take?"

BASIC PRINCIPLES

Put your customer at ease as soon as possible in the sales call.

Work at establishing a rapport with your customer. People like to do business with people they know on a personal level.

Consider every sales visit an opportunity to gather information that can help you.

Jot down the important information immediately after your call for future reference.

Early on, determine if the opportunity is real.

8

SELLING: PROBLEM SOLVING/CONSULTATIVE SELLING

The Top Performer succeeds because he understands two key points:

- Customers do not buy products/services, they buy solutions to business problems.

- In order to sell his product or service in the highly competitive environment of the '90s, he must position himself as a problem solver who has the solution to the customer's business problems.

The Average Performer often sells in one of two ways:

1. He sells on price only, that is, he bases his selling strategy on his ability to minimize the customer's overall purchase price. He tries to "low ball" the competition. With pure commodity selling, this is an effective strategy, but in systems selling, price is only one possible factor that influences a buying decision. (The Top Performer knows that customers will pay for features when those features solve a business problem and are priced commensurate with the perceived benefits.)

2. He sells product features, unaware that all the features in the world will mean nothing to his customers unless he positions them as solutions to the customer's business problems.

The ability to sell, using a problem-solving approach, can be applied to the simplest sales situations. Let's look at a number of simple sales situations that demonstrate how one can achieve improved sales results by focusing on the concept of selling solutions to customer problems.

Simple Sales and Problem Solving

The owners of a rug cleaning company sought help because they were having difficulty attracting new business.

"This is a highly competitive field. Is there any particular reason why someone should choose your company over any others?" I asked shortly into our meeting.

"We clean using 400 pounds of steam pressure and return 95 percent of the moisture to the holding tank."

"But how is that a benefit to the customer?"

I could tell that my question took them back, but they went on to explain that in heavy traffic areas, like commercial buildings, the combination of higher steam pressure and the 95 percent water return helped to force out and to pick up more dirt. Few of their competitors exceeded 300 pounds of pressure with a return of only 85 percent. My client's system resulted in a more thorough cleaning, which, over time, cut down on the frequency of cleanings.

Another benefit of the 95 percent water return was that the carpets were drier and could be walked on within three to four hours following treatments. They believed this was important to their business customers.

When I asked them to tell me what they told customers when they called on them, they repeated their initial statements about the higher steam pressure and the 95 percent water returns. But this meant nothing to the customer. The company had a competitive advantage but was failing to articulate it in a way that the customer could appreciate and understand. It was obvious that the owners did not think in terms of the customers' business problems.

We discussed several ways the owners could position their product. One possibility was to use their original technical explanation of the features: "We have 400 pounds of steam pressure and a 95 percent water return," but follow with an immediate explanation of the benefits of these features to the customers.

A second approach could be taken as follows:

"Many companies who have their carpets cleaned have two recurring complaints. The first is their carpets still look dirty after they've been cleaned. The second is that they have to be cleaned far too frequently. That's an expense they'd rather put off, so they wait until the carpets becomes noticeably grimy. Are these problems you now have?"

Most customers would answer yes, at which time the owners would then discuss why their equipment could do a better job and thus save the customer money.

"Which approach do you believe would get more sales," I finally asked them, "the one selling hardware features or the one selling customer benefits?"

In another case, the owners of a machine shop were having difficulty attracting new sales. A review of their brochure contained nothing that would lead me to believe that they were any different from any other shop. A discussion with the owners revealed more useful information:

1. They had a numerically controlled press that could handle material 60" x 72" in one operation. They told

me that there were not many presses of this caliber in the country.

2. They had equipment that made use of laser technology which allowed them to achieve tolerances of plus or minus 2/10,000 of an inch.

3. This same equipment allowed them to handle prototype work and short-run manufacturing orders faster and at less cost than competitive technologies.

Their brochure did not stress that they could handle the larger pieces, nor were they emphasizing these capabilities in their sales presentations. This company looked no different than any other machine shop competing for the same business.

It was clear that their marketing focus should be directed toward companies that needed a press that could handle large pieces, companies that required precision work that made the most of my clients' unique tolerance levels, and companies that required fast turnaround of a prototype and small-quantity orders. If the companies they called on did not have any one of these problems, my clients' time could better be spent elsewhere. They then changed their brochure and presentation to focus on the unique business problems they were solving.

Success in sales and/or marketing in simple sales situations like these can be measurably improved if one focuses attention on the customer's business problem and positions a product or service as a viable solution to those problems. The Top Performer understands this critical concept. In addition, he has internalized yet another critical concept to sales success, namely the importance of market segmentation.

Too often the Average Performer, who is busy selling products rather than solutions and benefits, fails to identify those customers whose business problems could best be solved with his particular product. In other words, he fails to maximize his selling time. He tries to sell to everyone. To succeed, it is important to make the most of your time by selecting those companies and/or industries for whom your product is best suited. Any Top Performer will tell you that market segmentation significantly increases the ratio of closes to calls.

Concept Selling

Before we discuss the problem-solving approach as it relates to the system-selling situation, it is important to understand what concept selling is.

Without a doubt, one of the great turnaround stories in American business is the Chrysler Corporation story. No doubt there are many reasons for the phenomenal turnaround of this company, but a key component involved Lee Iacocca's decision to go on the air and pitch Chrysler to the American public. What many people do not recognize is that he did not pitch specific models but pitched a concept instead—that is, extended warranties and a "Consumer's Bill of Rights" that enabled customers to return cars within a given time period, no questions asked. Iacocca knew that if the American public bought his concepts, they'd buy his cars.

Another interesting concept sale has been promoted by the Perrier company. They successfully conveyed the message that Perrier is an acceptable, if not avant-garde substitute for wine or liquor. In buying the concept, you purchase Perrier at a premium price over other sparkling waters that have been on the market for years.

Selling Top Management on the idea of factory automation and its long-term impact is another example of a concept sale. Selling robotics is the subsequent product sale.

Concept selling focuses on the broad implications of a purchase for a company. As such, its use truly positions the salesperson as a problem solver.

Problem Solving in the Systems Sale

A number of years ago, I held a position as Vice President of Marketing for a company selling electronic cash registers. The normal sell cycle for our products was between six and twelve months. At one point, we were in competition with one other vendor for a significant order (worth $3,000,000 per year) from a national retail chain. All other vendors had been eliminated.

Our competitor for this sale had a stand-alone cash register. Each register had its own logic and operated independently. If a register failed, the individual register could be replaced. On the other hand, we had a time-shared system; the registers were connected to two in-store controllers. If one controller (mini-computer) failed, the other controller took over. If both controllers failed, you could not ring up a sale, since the registers could not be operated independently. But this double failure situation had never occurred.

Let's look at the business problems that faced each department of this company, to see what part these issues played in the purchase decision and examine my company's sales strategies.

Merchandise Department

This potential customer was beginning to carry fashion merchandise. The company and, particularly, the Merchandise Department realized that, in order to be successful in this business, they needed timely and accurate fashion merchandise information. In our system, as each item was sold, the item number was keyed into the register, and that information was recorded on a magnetic tape on each controller. This gave the retailer the ability to poll one controller in each store after closing and transmit the day's merchandise sales information from that controller to a central computer location via the phone. Reports could then be generated in the evening and be on the buyers' desks at the beginning of the next business day. Our competitor had a magnetic tape on each register, but it was not feasible to poll each register in each store on a daily basis. Therefore, their system required that the magnetic tapes from each store be mailed in on a daily basis. It took up to three days to receive all the tapes for a given day at the computer center. Handling of these many tapes was cumbersome also.

Operations Department

This organization was more interested in the speed of customer check-outs and the ability to get in-store departmental totals available on demand. At this point, they were getting departmental totals by store the next day, but to compile the information into a form that was usable was a time-consuming and manually-intensive operation. As such, the information was not available on demand.

Since this retailer had a large number of stores, cost, maintenance, and reliability were also primary considerations to the Operations Department.

Finance Department

Initial purchase cost was this organization's major concern. The table below compares us and our competition with regard to solving those customers' problems. An "X" indicates who had the competitive edge. In those cases where neither had a competitive advantage, an "X" is shown for both.

Benefit	Us	Competition
Operations Department		
Speed of Check-Out	X	
Departmental Totals on Demand	X	
Reliability		X
Merchandise Department		
Accuracy of Information	X	X
Speed of Information	X	
Finance Department		
Initial Cost		X

Sales Strategies

Our sales strategies to this customer were as follows:

1. Sell the concept that success in fashion merchandising could not be achieved without daily merchandise information.

2. Gain concurrence that the benefits our equipment would provide would more than offset the major competitor's advantages of reliability and lower initial cost.

Strategy 1: Sell the concept that success in fashion merchandising could not be achieved without daily merchandise information.

To be successful in fashion merchandise a business must quickly identify what is selling, reorder it, identify what is not selling, and immediately mark it down. The need for quick reorders is essential because the fashion business is so seasonal, and manufacturers carry a limited inventory of materials.

First, we identified the two key players in the Merchandise Department who would be consulted prior to making the final decision. They were the Fashion Department head and the Vice President of Merchandise. It would be up to them to determine the importance of receiving timely merchandise information. It was critical that we make them see that their chances of success in this new endeavor would be greatly improved if they received this merchandise information overnight, as our system could supply, versus the two to three days that it might take if they chose our competitor's system.

Over time, we developed and gave them a number of case histories to demonstrate the benefits that could be gained from faster reporting of this information. We constantly posed the question of whether they could be competitive against department stores with three-day-old information, when the department store buyers were on the sales floor daily?

After much internal discussion they concluded that:

- The company could not meet forecasted growth without selling fashion merchandise.
- The company could not be successful in selling fashion merchandise without getting daily sales information.

Strategy 2: Gain concurrence that the benefits we provided more than offset the major competitor's advantages of reliability and lower initial cost.

Benefits can be tangible or intangible. An intangible benefit is one that cannot be quantified. For example, a customer might be willing to pay more for a car because a given dealership is located in a more convenient location to his home or business. The customer perceives value in that convenience. Many a system has been sold on intangible benefits based on a customer's perception of value. In some cases, these intangible benefits are strategic in nature and become far more significant to the sale than the tangible ones.

Tangible Benefits

We worked with both the Merchandise and the Operations organizations to develop data that clearly indicated the savings that could be realized by receiving information on fashion merchandise two days faster than the competition. All concurred that with the competitive system, markdowns on fashion merchandise could be reduced to eight percent of sales. With our system, that figure could be further reduced to seven percent.

Once these two departments saw the savings, we let them convince the Finance organization that our initial purchase price was no longer an issue. The savings that resulted from quicker markdowns more than offset the increased cost of our registers.

Other tangible benefits were the savings associated with the compilation of the in-store departmental totals and the speed of checking out customers. Our faster check-out meant that fewer registers and operators would be required.

Intangible Benefits

Despite the importance of the tangible benefits, this sales situation was one example where intangible benefits proved to be more important to the sale than the tangible ones.

Register reliability was a real concern to our customer. Though it had never happened, we had to admit that two controllers could conceivably fail, and if they did, a potential revenue loss could occur in a store that experienced such a double failure. This possibility was tempered by the fact that the company could lose the opportunity to be successful in the fashion business without timely fashion merchandise information.

With the Operations Department, we demonstrated the potential improvement in customer service that would go hand in hand with the faster check-out, that is, lines would be shorter. We also stressed the benefits that departmental totals on demand could provide, allowing for quick restocking in departments with high sales volumes. We asked them to focus on these benefits and what it meant to them from a profitability standpoint, rather than the hypothetical situation where two controllers would fail. They concluded that the benefits more than outweighed the risks.

As you might have guessed, we won the order. Let's briefly review why:

- We sold concepts and benefits, not price.
- We solved the customer's business problems.
- We identified the decision makers and influencers early and made sure all of them were aware of the benefits that our system could provide their company.
- We identified our champion, an individual within the company who was sold on our product, and provided him with all the information he needed to help us sell the system to his company.

Finding A Champion

A topic that was important to this sales situation, that I have not discussed, was the role of the champion. There are many selling situations where you will uncover a champion within the customer's company, a person who is enthusiastic about your product who will give you solid advice and assistance in selling the product. In this case a true champion was found within the Operations Department. This individual not only proved helpful in identifying the major influencers, but aided us in determining our sales strategy and how we could win over the other influencers and decision makers.

In those cases where the champion has the clout to make things happen, let him be your guide. Give him all the information he needs to help sell your proposal, and he will usually tell you the best way to proceed.

At this point, it is important that you also be aware of false champions. These are people who earnestly want to support you, but, in many cases, overestimate their influence or abilities to push your proposals through to closing. Don't ever assume that a sale is "in the bag" because of the assurances of a false champion. I cannot count the number of times I have heard someone say, "Pete is in our corner and he's the key decision maker" only to find that the competition did a better job of identifying and working with the true decision makers and influencers.

BASIC PRINCIPLES

Customers do not buy products/services, they buy solutions to business problems.

In the highly competitive environment of the next decade, you must position yourself as a problem solver who has the solution to your customer's business problems. Selling strategies should be focused toward problem resolution.

Customers will pay for features when those features solve a business problem and are priced commensurate with the perceived benefits.

Decision makers and influencers should be identified early in the sales process.

9

SELLING: PROPOSALS

The Good, the Bad, and the Technical

When I started to write this book, I went to several large companies to research some business proposals. I wanted to see how various businesses organized and presented their products to potential customers. The results surprised me.

Many business proposals were quite lengthy, contained voluminous details regarding product features, and were highly technical in nature. Others were not customer specific. These proposals might have succeeded in the 1970s and 1980s, but are not acceptable in the competitive environment of the 1990s where customers have little time and expect proposals to address their particular business problems.

One proposal dealt with the purchase of a large telephone system (PBX) that would require top management approval. The proposal was over one hundred pages long and spelled out the many product features in great detail. But most of the information was so technical that I could not understand it. I felt sure that top management wouldn't either, if they bothered to take the time to sift through all the data. Unfortunately, someone would have to read it carefully in order to understand the proposed features and to establish whether the features could address some of the company's problems.

To prove my point, try to decipher this portion, which appeared in The Executive Summary of the Proposal:

- Interchangeable system port interface module (PIM), system microprocessors, and universal port assignments provide unparalleled flexibility in accommodating system expansion and departmental relocations.
- Universal port assignments allow interchangeable circuit card slots, providing unlimited flexibility in card slot assignment and saving "real estate" in the system.
- System processors are redefinable in the control hierarchy, allowing for system growth without requiring costly changeout and replacement of system processing hardware.

Many managers don't know or care what a Port Interface Module is. Perhaps they are also in the dark about what unlimited flexibility in a card slot assignment would buy or what saving "real estate" in a system means. Can you imagine a busy top executive sifting through such a mess of technical jargon when his only question was "What can your product do for my business?"

Please don't misunderstand this criticism. I recognize that there is need for technical data in proposals, but a well thought out proposal places technical data in a section designated for a technician's reference. A simplified presentation that details what the proposed equipment could do for the customer should be placed up front, with technical discussions in the back.

This proposal, extensive though it was, made no attempt to identify the specific customer's business problems or explain how the feature-laden equipment would solve those problems.

Fortunately, during the course of my research, I found several proposals that were well written. One in particular was prepared for a hospital by a salesperson working for the same telecommunications company as the poor proposal we just examined. Where the first was lengthy, cumbersome, and difficult to read, this proposal was concise, specific, and clear. It quickly got to the point by delineating the customer's problems in a section entitled "Communication Systems Goals."

An excerpt from it follows:

COMMUNICATION SYSTEMS GOALS

The following goals have been compiled following meetings with key personnel.

1. Answering Position
   Configure the Northbrook answering position to be operated from Skokie at night.

2. Call Processing
   Allow outside calls to go directly to a department or room at both the Northbrook and Skokie locations.

3. Consolidation
   Consolidate modem and fax and/or other data lines to save on monthly network charges.

4. Cabling
   Explore alternatives to pulling new data cable as terminals are added at either location.

5. Growth
   Determine the current and expansion capacity of the two PBX systems. Outline viable options for continued growth.

This proposal clearly defined the customer's problems in terms that anyone could understand. Each of these goals (business problems) was then followed by a possible solution. For example:

Call Processing

Direct Inward Dial service could be implemented at Skokie and Northbrook. Your present system could be reprogrammed to allow each department to have its own number. We can change the programming at our central office to recognize the extra extensions.

Consolidation

Modem and fax lines can be consolidated at both locations to save on your monthly network expenses. Currently you are paying for 20 flat business lines at approximately $38 per line, per month ($760 per month total). If we assume that the modem and fax lines are in use only 40 percent of the time on average, and that at least 30 percent of the traffic is between locations that are directly serviced by the Skokie Central office, you could reduce your monthly network cost to $597.

It is interesting that in this proposal there were occasions when solutions were recommended that would not generate one penny of revenue to the telecommunications company making the proposal. Even more astounding were considerations of the possible shortcomings of the solutions that had been proposed by them.

For example, following the goal regarding the "Answering Position," a notation by the salesperson read:

There is a concern with this solution. Depending on the traffic into Northbrook at night, calls could quickly "stack up." The night bell would continue to ring until all calls waiting had been picked up. Emergency calls could end up ringing for long periods of time.

Here was a salesperson who took his role as a problem solver seriously. Not only did he address his customer's business problems head-on, but thoughtfully provided this potential customer with enough information to make the best business decision, even at the risk of sending the customer to a competitor.

A top executive would be impressed with this particular proposal. Unlike a wordy discussion of technical features, this proposal kept and held my attention. Who do you think would be more likely to get my business were it my decision?

Gaining Concurrence

There is an additional benefit to using this "problem - solution" format in a proposal. If the proposal is to be presented orally to the customer, as is often the case, this type of format lends itself to getting step-by-step agreement with your customer throughout the presentation. As each problem and solution is brought forward, the salesperson has an opportunity to get the customer's concurrence. This, in turn, assures him that he is "on the right track." This would be impossible with the first proposal, since I feel sure that the salesperson would, in all likelihood, end up spending a good part of the presentation explaining the technical jargon.

Presenting Proposals to the Customer

There are several approaches when submitting proposals to customers:

1. You can bring the proposal to the customer and review it with him at the time it is submitted.
2. You can mail it and set up an appointment to review it at a later date.
3. You can mail it and wait to respond to any questions he might have.

The Basic Elements of a Thorough Proposal

• Cover Letter

• Cover Sheet
  • Title (Example: "Voice and Data Communications Study")
  • Company for whom proposal is being prepared
  • Date prepared
  • Name of salesperson preparing proposal
  • Company submitting proposal

• Table of Contents
  1. Executive Summary
     An overview of the major points of the proposal
  2. Needs and Objectives
     A review of the customer's business problem and/or customer objectives
  3. Existing System and Service
  4. Detailed Recommendations
  5. Equipment
     The technical details of the proposed product and/or service, or an addendum in which the material is presented.
  6. Other
     Information regarding service, training, delivery, and installation details.
  7. Pricing, Payment, and Shipping Terms

Bringing the Proposal To The Customer

Most Top Performers prefer this method because it allows the salesperson to get immediate concurrence about the customer's business problems and immediate feedback regarding the solutions proposed. Perhaps less obvious is another advantage. This method enables the Top Performer to acquaint his customer with the layout, purpose, and key points of each section. The Top Performer knows that the proposal will probably be reviewed by other people as part of the decision-making process. By thoroughly acquainting his contact with the proposal, the Top Performer knows that his contact will be in a better position to discuss it and the product's merits with others intelligently. Last, but not least, the Top Performer recognizes that most people dislike dry reading. By presenting the material personally, the Top Performer is assured that his customer is familiar with all the key points and product strengths.

Mailing Proposals with Follow-up Presentations

Obviously, if the situation is such that you cannot review a proposal at the time that it is submitted, this second method is your next best alternative. However, you should be aware that, all too often, once the customer has read your proposal, he is not particularly receptive to a detailed presentation. Your attempts at explanation could be cut off by the customer response, "There's no need to take time on that section. I've read it and understand it."

Mailing Proposals and Answering Questions

My motto has always been: "If you don't have the time to present it, don't waste your time preparing it!" However, sometimes a customer will insist that he receive all proposals without formal presentations. In this case, I recommend that you have a short, but focused, summary at the beginning followed by sections on prices, service, technical information, etc. It is critical that you get your major points across quickly. The customer will probably read the first few pages and will only continue if he perceives that your proposal truly provides a viable solution to his problems.

BASIC PRINCIPLES

A good proposal:

• Is customer specific and identifies the customer's business problems.

• Details how the product solves those problems in easy-to-read customer's terms.

• Focuses on solutions, not product features.

10

SELLING:
HANDLING OBJECTIONS

Average Performers believe that customers raise objections only as they become more interested in a competitive product. They often do not know how to answer or address their customers' concerns effectively and thus become intimidated. They view the raising of the objections as confrontational. Consequently, they try to avoid situations where objections might be raised or openly discussed.

Top Performers realize that customers raise objections for many reasons, a degree of interest in a competitive product being only one. Unlike Average Performers, they actively encourage the discussion of objections.

Basically, there are three major reasons why a customer voices objections:

1. Interest in a competitive product
2. Need for additional information
3. The need to reinforce the correctness of their decision

Given a worst-case scenario, Top Performer recognizes that his only chance to turn the tide of a negative decision will come when his customer begins to articulate his concerns.

I prefer dealing with a customer who is open and honest with me. This type of customer lets me know where my company stands in the competition for the sale and at least gives me an opportunity to address his concerns.

Objections can just as easily be prompted by a simple need for additional information by the customer. When this is the case, the Top Performer knows that his open and calm response to his customer's statements and questions can sometimes be enough to put the issues raised to rest.

Top Performer also knows that some customers raise objections only after they have subconsciously made a buying decision. In this case, they raise the objections in order to elicit positive responses from the salesperson to reinforce the correctness of their decisions.

The Five Rules for Handling Objections

Top Performers adhere to five basic rules when confronted with objections.

Rule 1: Hear the customer out. Interrupt only to ask questions that will clarify the customer's objections and the reasons he is raising them.

Rule 2: Before responding to a customer's objection, make sure you have uncovered and understand ALL the objections he has at that time.

Rule 3: NEVER argue with a customer in response to an objection!

Rule 4: Overcome your customer's objections by using a questioning format to lead your customer into drawing his own conclusions.

Rule 5: Confirm that you have answered all the customer's objections.

Rule 1: Hear the customer out.

Your customer is an excellent source of competitive information. Let him talk. Let him tell you what you are up against. Interrupt only to ask questions that will clarify what you think you have heard.

NEVER assume that you know the reason for an objection!

> Customer: I like the NCR registers because they are stand alone.
>
> Average Performer (assumes he knows why the customer has raised this point and thinks to himself, "It's the reliability issue again"): We've never had a situation where both controllers have failed.
>
> Customer: I understand that. That isn't the source of my concern, but as long as you've brought it up, I do have a few questions on the way that the two controllers work together.
>
> (A lengthy discussion evolves on the controller operations.)

In this case, the Average Performer has made some hasty assumptions based on the customer's expressed preference for the NCR register. As we will see later, his assumption could be erroneous. However, in the process of trying to make a quick response to what he perceived to be the source of the customer's objection, he has brought the reliability issue to the forefront and set the conversation on a false course. The customer's train of thought has now been steered to a different topic. By interrupting his customer, AP lost the opportunity to get at the root of one of his customer's real concerns. The customer may or may not get around to verbalizing his initial concern again.

Let's examine how TP would handle the same situation.

> Customer: I like the NCR registers because they are stand alone.

Top Performer (assumes nothing and asks): What do you see as the advantage of the stand-alone feature?

Customer: I can move the registers wherever I have an electrical outlet in a store. With your system, I must prewire the register's location in order to tie them into the controllers. The stand-alone capability provides us with more flexibility which is important during the Christmas season.

Top Performer: I see. Is there anything else you like about the NCR system?

Customer: I like the adding machine format of their keyboard.

Top Performer: What do you like most about it?

Customer: It should be easier to train my people using the NCR keyboard because most people use adding machines. If we can train our employees to use a touch system, I believe the check-out of customers will go faster.

At this point, Top Performer's only goal was to elicit as much information as he could about the customer's concerns. He has done so quite effectively. Through patient and careful questioning, he uncovered valuable information that the Average Performer did not.

Let's examine yet another case to demonstrate the importance of hearing the customer out.

Customer: The information I have says the material used by your competition in their fiber optic connectors allows for tighter tolerances at higher temperatures. The variances on the hole sizes of their connectors is plus or minus 2 microns above 100 degrees Fahrenheit. Yours is plus or minus 4 microns.[9]

[9]Fiber optic connectors are used in the manufacture of cable assemblies. A cable assembly consists of a piece of fiber optic cable with a connector on each end. The variance in hole sizes in the connector has a significant impact on the quality of the cable assemblies. These assemblies are used to link various pieces of equipment optically, such as two computers linked for high speed data transfer.

Average Performer: That can't be! We use the same materials for the connectors.

Customer: Well, all I know is what I was told.

Average Performer (defensively): I don't know what they are trying to pull on you, but I'd check that again.

Once again, Average Performer's assumptions have drawn him to an erroneous conclusion. Once again, his assumptions have diverted his attention away from what should be his primary goal; to flush out his customer's true concerns.

In the same situation, Top Performer thinks to himself, "I thought we were using the same material as the competition, but says: "Do you happen to know what material they are using?"

Customer: I'd have to check the specs. Here they are. They are using Material M.

Top Performer: I see. I wasn't aware that they had made a change. Tell me, what do you see as the advantages to the tighter hole sizes?

Customer: We have a number of customers to whom we resell your connectors. They find they get less cable assembly rejections with the tighter tolerances.

Top Performer: Are you aware of any other advantages in Material M?

Customer: That's the only one that I'm aware of.

Rule 2: Before responding to a customer's objection, make sure you have uncovered and understand ALL the objections he has at that time.

The Top Performer puts this rule into practice by repeating what the customer has told him. In this way, he makes sure that he has understood the customer correctly, while encouraging the customer to discuss all his objections.

Top Performer: As I understand it, there are several features you prefer in the NCR register, specifically the stand-alone capability and their keyboard. Is that right?

Customer: Yes!

Top Performer: You like the stand-alone capability because it allows you the flexibility to move the registers to any location where you have an outlet.

Customer: You hit it on the head. It's an advantage during sale events since we can add more registers when and where we need them.

Top Performer: And you like the keyboard because you feel that it will make training faster and easier?

Customer: Yes! I assume that it will.

Top Performer: Are there any other features that the NCR offers that you prefer over ours?

In the case of the connectors:

Top Performer: Am I correct in understanding that you feel the improved tolerance offered by ABC's connectors is important to you because your customers will get less cable assembly rejections?

Customer: That's correct!

Top Performer: Are there any other features of the ABC product that you prefer over ours? (As a follow-up question) Do you have other concerns about our product?

Rule 3: NEVER argue with a customer in response to an objection!

If you begin with a confrontational attitude, the customer immediately becomes defensive and often feels a need to justify his position. All of us have a tendency to react in much the same way. Never tell a customer that he is wrong; acknowledge his point or opinion before you begin your response.

Recall the different reactions that the Average Performer and the Top Performer had to their customer's observation about the tolerance levels. The Average Performer became defensive and somewhat argumentative. Should he have found that the competition had used a different material, he would have had to backtrack with his customer. The Top Performer, who assumed nothing, concentrated on gathering more information before making any response.

Rule 4: Overcome your customer's objections by using a questioning format to lead him into drawing his own conclusions.

There are two distinct advantages to this format. First, the use of questions eliminates situations that might appear confrontational and argumentative. Second, this approach provides greater flexibility, allowing the salesperson to take a number of possible approaches in overcoming customer objections and leading the customer into agreement.

Top Performer: ABC's tolerances are better at higher temperatures and should give you fewer cable assembly rejections. The reason has to do with the unique properties of Material M. However, Material M does have disadvantages, namely, that it becomes brittle when used with certain epoxies. Do you have applications for the connectors where the temperature will be above 100 degrees?

Customer: We have some applications down south in the summer where the temperatures reach that.

Top Performer: What percentage of your purchases will require the tighter tolerances?

Customer: Oh! Less than 10 percent, I'd guess.

Top Performer: May I assume that you are still considering us as a viable vendor for the remaining 90 percent?

Customer: Yes. Under 100 degrees, you and ABC have the same tolerances.

In this actual case, the Top Performer continued to use a questioning format to elicit information in a way that was nonthreatening, but led his customer into drawing a favorable conclusion.

Top Performer: You indicated that you sell the connectors to third parties. Is that correct?

Customer: That's right.

Top Performer: Do you have any control over the types of epoxy they use?

Customer: Even though we give them specifications, I wouldn't know if they follow our recommendations.

Top Performer: I know how that is. They get a rush job and use any material they have available. What happens if there is a connector problem? Who do they turn to?

Customer: They always come back to us, even if the problem is theirs.

Top Performer: We've found the same thing. Could the fact that ABC's product becomes brittle with certain epoxies present you with a potential field problem?

Customer: I never really thought about it, but it certainly could.

Let's assume that the customer has told TP that he does not foresee a problem with the third parties since they adhere to the specs. How would he respond?

Top Performer: You are fortunate. We found that as we expanded our base and began dealing with smaller companies, we encountered problems we hadn't anticipated.

The advantage of our product is that it eliminates any problems if a customer does use the wrong epoxy. This capability costs you nothing. I guess you might call it an insurance policy.

The Top Performer has given the customer something to think about. During TP's next visit, he would ask about this issue again.

> Top Performer: Larry, the last time we met I mentioned the advantage our product material has over material M. Specifically, our product can be used with all epoxies. You indicated that you didn't see this as a problem. Have you considered the advantage that our product could offer you as you expand your customer base?

Should the customer not see this as an advantage, TP is no worse off than he was before.

If you do not have an immediate answer to an objection, you are better off telling the customer that you'll get back to him regarding his concern. Too often, salespeople feel that if they put out enough information, something will work. Don't try to bluff your customer. You lose credibility with this approach and tarnish your image as a problem solver.

> Top Performer: The use of Material M in ABC's connectors is relatively new. Let me find out if we have any information on it. (or "Let me find out if we have any comparisons between what we are using and material M.")

In the case of the registers:

> Top Performer: Your issue on the keyboard is a good one. There must be a reason why we designed ours the way we did, but I'm not sure what it is. Let me find some information about it and get back to you the next time we meet.

It would be irresponsible to suggest that you can always answer all your customer's objections to their satisfaction. Sometimes, the competition has a real advantage that can't be denied. Don't try. In these situations, it is important that you end on a positive note, reinforcing those product features/benefits that can solve other critical customer business problems.

For example:

Top Performer: I realize that you still feel that the stand-alone capability is important for you. However, I would like you to keep in mind the advantages that my product offers, namely . . .

Rule 5: Confirm that you have answered all the customer's objections.

Any number of concluding questions can ensure that you have covered all your bases.

"Larry, have I answered all your questions?"
"Is there anything I have not covered to your satisfaction?"
"Are there any other open issues?"

BASIC PRINCIPLES

Customers raise objections for the following reasons:

- Because they are interested in a competitive product.

- They have a need for additional information.

- To reinforce the correctness of their decision.

The five rules for handling objections are:

- Rule 1
  Hear the customer out. Interrupt only to ask questions that will clarify the customer's objections and the reasons he is raising them.

- Rule 2
  Before responding to a customer's objection, make sure you have uncovered and understand ALL the objections he has at that time.

- Rule 3
  NEVER argue with a customer in response to an objection!

- Rule 4
  Overcome your customer's objections by using a questioning format to lead your customer into drawing his own conclusions.

- Rule 5
  Confirm that you have answered all the customer's objections.

11
SELLING: CLOSING

Countless books and articles have been written on the subject of closing. However, I have some real concerns with the messages many of them try to promote. Some authors, especially those in the consumer selling area, view closing as a sly game in which a naive customer is pitted against a stereotypic "smooth talking" salesperson. The authors try to arm their readers with a thousand verbal gimmicks, all meant to trick and/or push customers into purchase decisions. I would hate to think that any of my customers ever felt that I had fooled, pressured, or cajoled them into a purchase decision. I would like to think that my customers considered their decisions to buy from me the natural and wise course that followed my efforts to solve their business problems.

I have no doubt that these high-pressure sell approaches could be successful in some consumer situations. Sometimes, a salesperson may only have one or possibly two chances to "hook and close" a customer before he walks out the door. But I seriously question whether these techniques have any value beyond their ability to "win the moment." They are of no use to the salesperson who hopes to establish a sincere, honest, and long-standing business relationship with a customer, since these techniques have a tendency to make a customer feel uncomfortable and harassed.

These same approaches, however, are downright disastrous in the systems selling environment. The majority of systems customers are savvy business people who would be highly insulted and offended by anything resembling closing chicanery. A salesperson employing the kind of shallow, "shoot-from-the-hip" tactics promoted in many of these books would, in all likelihood, be "out on his ear" in no time. The systems customer is a sophisticated and astute decision maker who demands professionalism and respect from those he/she deals with. Secondly, the systems sell cycle is such that a salesperson has many meetings and discussions with his potential customers before an order is given. Shallow, "con" tactics are difficult to sustain over long periods of time, even with naive customers.

Not all of the books that are available encourage this type of salesmanship, of course. Some of the available literature on selling contain useful techniques that are both ethical and sound. Unfortunately, very few deal with the specific sales challenges associated with systems selling.

At first I hesitated to insert a separate chapter on closing. I did not want to promote the commonly held belief that the skills to close were something separate and apart from the rest of the skills needed in the sales process. They aren't. Closing does not require any unique skills. If you are disciplined and diligent in following the advice given thus far, you will find that closing is the natural culmination of your business relationships with your customers.

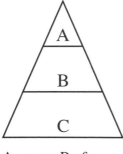

Average Performer

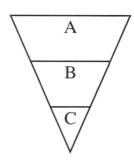

Top Performer

As you may recall from Chapter 6, A represents the fact-finding or fact-gathering part of the selling process. B represents the amount of time that should be devoted to moving the customer along in the selling process, and C represents the time that should be given to closing.

Top Performers understand the need for taking time in A and B. They spend most of their time developing a rapport with their customers, establishing and defining their customers' needs and problems, and positioning their products as the solutions to those problems. Where Average Performers move rapidly through steps A and B and barrel headlong toward C, Top Performers know that time spent in A and B will make closing (C) come naturally. As such, closing is more an evolutionary than revolutionary part of the selling process.

Craig Y., a Vice President of Sales for a Fortune 100 company, one of the many people I interviewed when researching this book, took this reasoning one step further. He maintained that salespeople would always have difficulty closing if "they did not get agreement through every step of a sale." He also believed that, given customer concurrence, closing should be a natural conclusion to the sales process.

We briefly touched on this idea of "getting concurrence" in the discussion of proposals. However, it is an important concept worth emphasizing. By getting concurrence from a customer at each step, the Top Performer is assured that he is always on the right track, especially when trying to identify and solve his customer's problems. The Average Performer does not usually recognize that he needs this agreement.

Getting Concurrence or Agreement in a Presentation

One of the reasons I took such pleasure in reading the proposal that included the list of "Communication System

Goals" (Chapter 9) was that the writer's format seemed so conducive to seeking and getting immediate concurrence from the customer. Identifying and listing the goals of a customer in a presentation or proposal naturally lend themselves to a discussion of whether the goals are "on the mark." As I read this proposal, I could see the presentation following a natural course. He could state the goals he had gathered from his talks with key decision makers and influencers and follow with questions that would help elicit responses from his customers:

> "Do you agree that the goals I have listed sum up your objectives in seeking a new telecommunications system?"
>
> or
>
> "Do you agree with the goals I've stated? Are any of them misstated? Have I left anything out?"
>
> or
>
> "Have I stated your goals correctly? Is there anything I've missed?"

By receiving the customer's "yes" he would be getting concurrence during his presentation and providing himself with all the information he would need to sell that customer on his product. Had he missed any key issues, these questions would give the customer the opportunity to voice his goals and/or concerns.

It is important that the questions you ask to prompt the customer's response not appear rhetorical. Pausing after each one will let your customer know that you expect and want his input.

If you fail to get agreement on the goals of your customer or, at the very least, fail to uncover a working definition of his business problems, the most eloquent proposal in the world will prove meaningless to him.

Do you recall the wordy proposal that referred to the Port Interface Module (Chapter 9)? Can you imagine how meaningless that proposal must have appeared to the customer and how difficult it would have been to get his concurrence on any of the goals the way they were stated? Such proposals and presentations are rarely able to elicit a customer's honest and immediate agreement.

> Salesperson: Do you agree that our Port Interface Module will provide you with unparalleled flexibility in accommodating your system expansions or departmental relocations?

> Customer: Huh?

Most customers are hesitant to tell you if they do not understand your proposal. Do not make your customer sift through the information you give him to find out if the product you are selling addresses his problems.

Once you have obtained agreement on the customer's goals and problems, the next step is to propose your solutions and get agreement. You might follow your proposed solutions with questions like:

> "Do you believe we've adequately addressed the problems?"
>
> or
>
> Do you feel that our solutions will help you accomplish your objectives?"

If through discussion, your customer provides you with goals you had not originally anticipated, be sure to follow up with an updated proposal that includes those new goals and the solutions you propose.

The "No Means Yes" Close

You now feel confident that you have addressed all the customer's concerns and believe that the decision makers and influencers are satisfied and leaning toward your product. It's time to ask for the order.

An effective technique used by many Top Performers is the "No Means Yes" close. Using this technique, the Top Performer simply summarizes what has been proposed and agreed upon. Further, this technique is useful in: (1) Flushing out any unaddressed concerns, and (2) Reaffirming to the customer the correctness of his decision to purchase from you. In the conversation that follows, the final "no" actually means "yes."

> Top Performer: Let's recap where we stand. We have identified the following business problems:
>> 1. ....
>> 2. ....
> Is that correct?
> Customer: That's correct.
> Top Performer: Let's briefly review our proposed solutions to these problems:
>> 1. ....
>> 2. ....
> Are you satisfied with these solutions?
> Customer: Yes, I am.
> Top Performer: You expressed the following technical concerns which I believe we addressed:
>> 1. ....
>> 2. ....
> Have we addressed all your technical issues and are you satisfied with our responses?
> Customer: Yes, I'm satisfied.
> Top Performer: I believe that your Service Manager is pleased with our proposal to service the equipment and the terms of our service contract.

Customer: He is.

Top Performer: Given that our product solves your business problems, meets your technical specifications, meets your service requirements, and is within your price range, is there any reason why we should not proceed with the sale?

or

Top Performer: Given that our product solves . . . can you think of any reason why we shouldn't move ahead with a purchase order at this time?

At this point, the customer will either place the order or tell you of other reservations or concerns.

There will always be some salespeople who will still be squeamish about asking for an order directly. For those people may I suggest yet another approach.

Timid Tom: Given that our product solves . . . where do we go from here, or what do you see as your next step?

Matching Corporate Resources

Fred H. never called on either the technical or corporate support personnel to help him with his accounts. Fred thought that a request for help would be a poor reflection on his ability. Interestingly enough, Fred's customers did not see it quite the same way. One of Fred's customers told me:

"You're the first person I've met from your company besides Fred. I was beginning to believe that he was the only one working for your company!" It was apparent that this particular customer felt slighted and had not been handled very well. However, his comment effectively demonstrates an important point.

Sometimes a sale requires technical support or even top management intervention. Top Performers are quick to assess when and where corporate resources are needed to close a sale or serve a customer and do not hesitate to ask for them.

They are mature enough to recognize that a request for assistance is not a poor reflection on their ability. Average Performers are often reluctant to ask for support of any kind.

When I was the General Manager of a division at General Instruments, one of our target accounts was a midwest telephone company. We felt sure that a sale to them would give us credibility with other telephone companies. Even though Phil B., our salesperson, was qualified to answer most of the questions that telephone company might raise, we automatically provided Phil with support. If the company told us that their technical people would be at a given meeting, we brought in our technical support people. If the company requested a meeting to discuss service, we made sure that our service manager was in attendance. Why did we bother?

As I have stated before, people like to do business with others with whom they are comfortable and know. Service personnel like to talk to service people. Technically oriented people like to talk to technical support people. They speak the same language and have mutual interests. This relationship among business peers should be nurtured and fostered. If there is a problem, the customer then feels comfortable and confident enough to phone his peer, knowing that the person on the other end will be responsive.

Despite this support, Phil continued to have difficulty getting to the ultimate decision maker, Joe M., a vice president at the midwest firm. The person who was heading the team to evaluate our product was reluctant to give Phil access to Joe. Phil told his contact that I, the general manager, was coming to town and would like to have lunch with his boss. Because of my position, I had access to levels in the organization that Phil did not and they accepted the invitation. Of course, prior to the meeting, Phil updated me on the account, stressing the customer's business problem and how our equipment could help the company.

Through the coming months, I saw Joe two more times. I took advantage of these occasions to find out about his "hot buttons" and to acquaint him with how our product could solve their company's business problems. Thanks to Phil's appropriate utilization of corporate resources and his effective management of the account, we got the order.

"It Ain't Over Till It's Over"

Steve G. had been kept waiting for his 10 o'clock appointment for over an hour. The President finally appeared.

"I'm sorry I kept you waiting," he apologized, "but we have decided to buy our electronic cash registers from NCR."

Steve was more than a little disturbed. "My company's paid for the trip. At least you could listen to what I have to say about our product?"

"I'm really sorry, but I haven't got the time. I am going to my lawyer's office to review and sign the contract right now," the President told him as he walked toward the door. "I suppose you can ride along with me if you'd like."

Steve jumped at the offer. In the following thirty minutes, Steve convinced the President to listen to his whole presentation. An hour later, I received a call from Steve, who was in the President's lawyer's office. They wanted to discuss a contract for the purchase of our electronic registers.

An unusual case? You bet! But, there is a moral to this story and Yogi Berra couldn't have said it better. "It ain't over till it's over."

Top Performers realize that the closer a customer comes to making a decision the more time you MUST spend with him. In this case, the NCR salesperson should have been with the president. His absence at a critical time was the crack in the door that allowed Steve to win the order.

I can't tell you the number of times I have seen a forecast projecting an expected order from a major customer within thirty days, but the salesperson's calendar didn't show a single visit scheduled.

When I talk to salespeople about this, their usual response is, "It's in the bag! All that's required is a final signature."

My immediate comeback is, "and what do you think the competition is doing right now? Conceding defeat? Don't you believe that they are pulling out all the stops to turn that customer's decision around?"

Your motto should be, "RUN SCARED." Never assume that you are winning. Assume you are losing. Then you will take the steps necessary to guarantee the victory.

"Goodyear's most humbling moment came about two years ago when GM named Firestone the exclusive tire supplier for its futuristic Saturn models. The contract, which called for one million tires a year, was seen in the auto industry as an endorsement of Firestone's leading-edge tire technology.

Apparently convinced it would be chosen, Goodyear hadn't courted GM as aggressively as Firestone, which took GM through its most modern and only non-union plant in Wilson, North Carolina. Goodyear showed GM through an aging plant in Tennessee, not its state-of-the-art facility in Lawton. "We flat-out lost," acknowledged Robert E. Mercer, former chairman."[10]

---

[10]Stricharchuk, Gregory, "Embattled Giant: Goodyear Squares Off To Protect Its Turf From Foreign Rivals," *The Wall Street Journal,* December 29, 1989, p. B1.

The only way to guarantee that you will get the order is to be there.

> Customer: Well, TP. It looks like the paperwork should be signed next week.
>
> Top Performer: That's great! Why don't I come down Monday and be available to answer any last minute questions.
>
> Customer: That isn't necessary.
>
> Top Performer: I planned to be in your area anyway. It's no problem for me to stop in then.

The Top Performer will make sure that he touches base with the key players, just to make sure that nothing has or will happen to derail the order.

The Stall

It is important to be mindful of another closing mistake. *If the committed date for an order keeps getting pushed back, there is a strong possibility that your order is in trouble.* Again, the motto is "Run Scared!" and put on a full court press. The longer you wait to do this, the higher the probability that you will not get the order. Get to the customer to find out what the problem is.

Roy was renegotiating a contract with the S Company, the company's largest customer. The contract negotiations kept dragging. Roy wasn't worried. Who could the S company buy from but his company? The only other major supplier of the product was also a competitor of the S company. Surely, they wouldn't buy from them. Besides, Roy had worked up new pricing that was less than the present contract. The longer the S company delayed, the more money Roy's company made.

Approximately two months after negotiations began, Roy got a call from the S company. They had decided to split their business between his company and the competition.

"By the way," they told Roy, "The price we are getting from them is much lower than what you offered us."

Roy not only lost over $500,000 in business, but saw the margins on any new business in the future eroding.

The expression, "You've got to get the order off the street" is so very true. In this case, the order should not have been "on the street" in the first place. Roy should have moved quickly to secure a new contract.

As a contract signing or award keeps dragging, there are three things that could be happening. Two of them are bad news.

1. You've got the order, but paperwork is holding things up. Customers will often tell you this, but only sometimes is it true. Check it out.
2. The order is about to be split between you and your competition.
3. The competition is on the move and is in the process of getting the order.

BASIC PRINCIPLES

If you consistently get agreement through every step of the sale, closing becomes the natural culmination of the sales process.

"It Ain't Over Till It's Over."

The closer the customer gets to a decision, the more time you must spend with that customer.

Remember the best tip of all, "ALWAYS RUN SCARED!"

12

SERVICING:
SERVICE

In a *Wall Street Journal* article, Thomas Arenberg of Arthur Andersen and Co. declared, "Better than 50% of [companies] are saying they have to get closer to their customers, while only 5% to 10% are doing the work it takes to get there."[11]

At the same time, a whopping 68 percent of the customers who recently changed the companies with whom they did business, admitted that they had made the changes, not because they were dissatisfied with the products (13 percent) of their former vendors, but because an employee of that company had shown "an attitude of indifference" toward them.[12]

No company or salesperson can afford to be lulled into a false sense of security based on the mistaken belief that customers will continue to do business out of loyalty or because they have no other place to go. Nothing could be further from the truth, especially in these competitive times. Customer loyalty is born of satisfaction, not desperation; a fact that is clearly demonstrated in this study. Good customer service has always, and will always, make good business sense.

[11]Amanda Bennett and Carol Hymowitz, "For Customers, More than Lip Service?" *The Wall Street Journal,* October 6, 1989, p. B1.
[12]Mortgage Banking, June 1987

The Customer's Expectations

TO MY CUSTOMERS

MY BELIEF: CUSTOMERS DON'T CARE HOW MUCH I KNOW
UNTIL
THEY KNOW HOW MUCH I CARE!

MY PURPOSE: TO COMPETE FOR THE PRIVILEGE
OF SERVING YOUR NEEDS![13]

Don, a Top Performer, put this credo on the front of every one of his proposals. Does this sound like a salesman who was service-oriented? You bet! It wasn't just good public relations rhetoric either. Don was committed to this purpose, believed in it, and lived up to it. I know. I was his boss.

I can recall several instances where Don demonstrated his commitment to his customers. At one point, Don had promised to have a proposal ready for a customer by 9 A.M. on a Monday morning. His travel schedule had been heavy, and he was ticketed for a flight to another part of his territory early that same morning. With the help of his wife, Don worked over the weekend, finished the proposal, and drove two hours on Sunday evening to deliver it to the company's guard shack as he'd promised. He confirmed its arrival to the customer with a call from the airport Monday morning. Don truly earned the privilege to serve his customers and consistently demonstrated how much he cared for them.

Another Top Performer once put it this way: "Servicing an account means that you have to be willing to go that extra mile for your customer. You must be willing to sell your customer's ideas and requirements to your own people. You'll get the door slammed in your face, but the extra effort is what the customer expects from you."

[13]Don Wheeler, Raleigh, NC

This Top Performer related an incident when a customer had requested a design change on a product they were buying. Tony had tried to go through the normal channels to initiate the change, but had been turned down. As a Top Performer, he had made a point of developing a good relationship with the engineers in his company over the years. As he could not influence the marketing people, he talked to one of the engineers who thought the request was a good idea and could be easily implemented. With the engineer to back him up, Tony approached the marketing department again. Reluctantly, they agreed to the change.

These two Top Performers clearly understood what a customer's service expectations are. Quite simply:

> A customer expects that you will respond to his requests (regarding pricing information, product modifications etc.) and will attempt to find solutions to his problems within the time frames to which you have committed. Further, he expects to be kept abreast of the progress and status of his situation.

To the customer you are the company, and to the company you represent the customer. It's not always a comfortable position, but one in which the Top Performer again sets himself apart from his peers. In servicing his customers he demonstrates:

- Knowledge—The Top Performer understands how to use the resources of the company and knows who to go to when there is a problem. He takes the time to get to know and maintain good working relationships with these resources.

- Tenacity—The Top Performer never gives up until all possible approaches have been exhausted.

• Responsibility—The Top Performer makes himself the key point of contact for his customer. This does not mean that other members of other organizations do not talk to his customers, but the Top Performer makes sure that he is kept apprised of what is going on and what will be said to his customers. He is always in a position to communicate to customer management what is being done to address a complaint or request. As the single point of contact, he may delegate activities, but not responsibility for the customer's problems and requests.

• Follow-up—The Top Performer makes sure that the commitments he makes are met.

The Worst Mistake You Can Make

Without a doubt, the worst mistake you can make is to tell a customer that you will get back to him within a given period of time and then fail to do it! Of course, you probably have an excuse. Someone that you called for information has yet to get back to you, right? So you haven't got the answers for your customer yet. That may very well be true, but why is your response to let your customer sit and stew? Do you really think someone else's failure to call you back justifies your failure to meet the commitments you've made?

My wife and I recently moved into a new home. As is often the case, we immediately set to work on several projects, the first being the paving of our driveway and the second being the purchase of a dining set. Knowing that we would be entertaining friends for Thanksgiving, we were anxious to have both projects completed by the beginning of November. We contracted for the paving and ordered the dining set with assurances that it would be delivered before Thanksgiving.

Several weeks passed. As the date for the delivery of the table and chairs neared, my wife called to check the status of the order. The front office had no record of our order. With Thanksgiving just a few weeks away and a house full of guests arriving, my wife was more than a little upset. The saleswoman sensed this and quickly promised to have a manager call her back that same day.

The phone at our home rang ten minutes later, and an apologetic manager promised to look into the matter. I will confess that neither my wife nor I had much faith that we would have a place for our guests to sit and eat Thanksgiving dinner, and were tempted to cancel the order. But the manager assured us that he would do everything he could to find a set at another store. This didn't happen overnight. In fact, it took two weeks to locate an acceptable set. All the while, the manager diffused our frustration and anger with frequent calls to update us on his search. We felt comforted by his calls and the knowledge that he was working on the problem. He continued to call right up to the day that the table and chairs were delivered.

On the other hand, the paving situation went quite differently. Soon after the paving was completed, I noticed some cracks in the new driveway and called the paver. I left a message asking him to come out and inspect the cracks and call me back. Several days went by with no response from him. I began to get quite agitated and repeatedly called, leaving several messages on his answering machine. Still, there was no response. After several weeks with no call back, I left a scathing message. I was fully prepared to take him to small claims court when he finally called back. He had, in fact, inspected the driveway weeks before. Unfortunately, he had never informed me. He had determined that repair was in order and had made plans to fix the cracks, but he failed to keep me apprised of his plans. Consequently, I was more than a little skeptical and insisted on a specific date for the repairs. Here was a very different case. This businessman had alienated me as a customer and a potential reference and all for want of one customer call back.

At home or in the office, we're all the same. None of us likes to be left hanging. At the very least, leaving your customer stewing creates unnecessary anger, friction, and rigidity. At the very worst, it can send your customer packing. The wise salesperson remembers that customers are far more flexible, reasonable, and willing to compromise if they are routinely kept informed and assured that someone is looking out for their interests. Studies conducted by the P.I.M.S. Strategic Planning Institute indicate that 95 percent of customers will do business with you again if you resolve a problem immediately.

I have always made it a habit to return all my customer calls within twenty-four hours. It's just good business and common courtesy to give your customer a call back, even if you have nothing new to report. He needs to be kept informed of what is happening and what you are doing to solve his problem.

> Top Performer: Tom, I know I said I'd have an answer for you today. Unfortunately, I still don't. It looks like it's more complicated than I had anticipated. Let me explain what we are doing to find out about_____.
>
> Would it be all right if I call you tomorrow with an update on our progress? Hopefully, I'll have more information then.

It is important for you to avoid the temptation to blame other departments for any delays in responding to your customer. Blaming another organization might take the heat off you personally, but it positions your company poorly. Remember that the customer is doing business with your company as a whole. Putting the blame on someone else may help you win the battle, but in the end, your company may lose the war.

The same principle applies to potential customers. A prompt call back can make or break a sale. The failure to call back a potential customer when you say you will sends an especially stinging message.

"If he can't get back to me before he makes the sale, why should I believe that he'll take care of me after the sale!"

"When Motorola was supplying microprocessors for Steve Job's new 'Next' computer, George Fisher, President and Chief Executive of the Schaumberg, Illinois, company, made a point of returning Mr. Job's frequent calls within five to ten minutes. 'We showed we not only could help him, but we were interested in his business,' Mr. Fisher says."[14]

Since last year, Motorola executives have even been required to carry pagers.

Maintaining Your Customer Base

By now you know how many cold calls it takes to get a suspect and how many suspects you contact before you find a prospect. You know how much time and energy it takes to sign that prospect. Put a dollar figure on your efforts. The old adage holds true. "It is cheaper to maintain a customer than it is to sign a new one."

Mitch L. had just joined a data communications company as their Vice President of Marketing. It was a small but successful start-up company with only two salespeople and

[14]Amanda Bennett and Carol Hymowitz, "For Customers, More than Lip Service?" *The Wall Street Journal*, October 6, 1989, p. B1.

a Director of Sales. Soon after joining, he decided to make a personal visit to each of the company's Original Equipment Manufacturers to introduce himself and to find out if there was anything he might do.

The first company he visited was his second largest customer. He was led into a conference room where he fully expected to meet one or two of the key players. To his shock, six people from four different departments were waiting for him, and none of them looked particularly happy.

For the next hour and a half they let Mitch have it. They didn't mince any words in letting him know just how unresponsive his company had been to their needs in the past. The marketing department had been crying for software enhancements to make their products competitive but had received no word on when or if the additions could be made. The engineering department was frustrated over existing software problems that Mitch's company had failed to address. The increase in service calls resulting from this problem was costing the customer money. The purchasing department was disgusted with the poor delivery performance.

Unfortunately, variations on the same theme followed Mitch as he made his way to each of the remaining customers. It was clear that the sales organization had neglected the existing accounts in their pursuit of new accounts. It was also clear that the president had not taken his customers' threats to take their business elsewhere seriously.

With a greeting like that, Mitch couldn't help but take notice and action. He immediately reassigned one of his two salespeople to serve the two largest accounts. These two customers accounted for 60 percent of the company's business. He quickly got agreement from the president to hire a new salesperson to service the other existing accounts.

He set up meetings with the customers and prepared lists detailing the software problems. These problems were then prioritized by the customers. Target dates for the solution of each of the problems were scheduled. The lists were updated on a regular basis and progress was charted. In addition, customers were informed of the status of deliveries on a weekly basis.

Unfortunately, Mitch found himself in a reactive position with many of his customers for a long while. But as the customer problems were resolved and communications between Mitch's company and his customers improved, the focus of his meetings slowly shifted away from the short-term problems, which the customers now knew he would handle, to the more long-term issues of product needs and enhancements.

Mitch's company had been headed for disaster. Without Mitch's intervention, I have no doubt they would have lost most of their existing customers. More than likely, that would have eventually put them out of business. In their push to acquire new customers, Mitch's company had forgotten one of the most elementary facts of business, i.e. "IT IS CHEAPER TO MAINTAIN A CUSTOMER THAN IT IS TO SIGN A NEW ONE."

The Value of Periodic Meetings

Holding periodic meetings with all of your customers, as Mitch did, is a healthy routine to establish. These meetings give your customers a chance to discuss any issues and concerns and effectively prevents the kind of pent-up and explosive situations that Mitch witnessed in his first meetings with his customers. It also proves useful in giving you an opportunity to sniff out new revenue possibilities.

Prior to each meeting, prepare an agenda based on customer input, and forward a copy to the customer in advance. During the meeting, document what is said, including all "action items" whether they be yours or the customers, with the names of those who are responsible for seeing them through. Forward a copy of this documentation to the customer shortly after the meeting.

It is important to note that outstanding action items should be reviewed at every meeting. This review provides an orderly format to ensure that all the customer's problems are addressed and satisfactorily resolved.

Executive Visits

I am a strong proponent of executive visit programs, especially as they relate to servicing major accounts. They are one of the key elements that separates Top Performing companies from the crowd. I consider executive visit programs a kind of preventive medicine in that they are proactive rather than reactive. Too many companies only send corporate executives to visit an account when there are problems.

Imagine the positive impact if your customers were to receive a call from you stating your intention to set up a top level meeting whose only purpose would be to thank them for their business and review areas where your company could improve service to them.

BASIC PRINCIPLES

A customer expects that you will respond to his requests (regarding pricing information, product modifications etc.) and will attempt to find solutions to his problems within the time frames to which you have committed. Further, he expects to be kept abreast of the progress and status of his situation.

It is cheaper to maintain a customer than it is to sign a new one.

The worst mistake you can make is to tell a customer that you will get back to him within a given period of time and then fail to do it.

13

SERVICING:
TRADE SHOWS

Working the Shows

Walk into any hotel restaurant or bar during any trade show and scan the room. If it's after five, you're bound to see a lot of salespeople. "So what?" you ask. "It doesn't take a genius to figure that out."

You're absolutely right! But what would you say if I told you that I could scan that room and probably pick out the Top Performers? Now that would be something, wouldn't it?

"Come on. How could you do that? What would you look for?" you ask.

It's really quite simple. I look for the salesperson who is with a customer. While the Average Performer has called it a day and is busy dining with his peers, the Top Performer has seized one of the great opportunities offered at any show, the chance to meet with customers and prospects. The Top Performer knows that trade shows are teeming with key customers and good prospects. He is not about to let the opportunity to acquire new business or cement the relationships he has with existing customers and corporate executives pass him by. Weeks before, he planned and scheduled as many breakfast, lunch, and dinner meetings as he could with people he knew would be in attendance.

Show Booths

An important feature of the trade show is the show booth. But, there is nothing more irritating than walking into a show booth to find all the reps talking amongst themselves. The potential customer, who may or may not have the time to wait until a conversation is over, is made to feel like an intruder instead of like the welcomed and expected guest he should be. Years ago, I made a point of designating someone manning the booth as a greeter. This responsibility was rotated throughout the day. Having a greeter ensures that no one walks through the booth unnoticed or ignored. As a person enters the booth, the greeter goes over and says, "Welcome to our booth! My name is _____. Is there anything you would like to see in particular?" If the person is interested in a specific product line, the greeter then escorts him over to the individual who is giving the demonstration and introduces the potential customer.

BASIC PRINCIPLES

Make maximum use of your time at trade shows to meet customers and prospects.

Designate one person as a greeter at your show booth.

PART II

HOW TO BECOME A TOP-PERFORMING
SALES MANAGER

14

THE SALES MANAGER'S ROLE: SUPER CLOSER?

"One of the greatest failings of today's executive is his inability to do what he's supposed to do."

Malcolm Kent

A good friend of mine was recently promoted to district manager and took over an existing territory in the Midwest. During his initial territory visit, Roger recognized that one of his salespeople lacked what he considered solid closing skills. "How much time did Pete (the previous district manager) spend with you?" he asked.

"He traveled with me at least once a month and spent two to three days with me during each visit."

Surprised, Roger decided to dig a little deeper.

"How much time did Pete spend discussing areas where you might improve your closing skills?"

"Closing skills? We didn't spend any time on closing skills. When I went on a sales call with Pete, he just took over the meetings."

Like so many sales managers, I believe that Pete saw his job as that of a "Super Closer." I will even go so far as to bet that Pete believed that his example would be enough to improve the young man's closing skills over time. He had fallen prey to what I call the "Super Closer Syndrome."

Another new sales manager once admitted to me that he spent five days a week on the road, crisscrossing his district in an attempt to participate in every aspect of his sales staffs' proposals to customers. He became personally involved in the closing of all the sales that his salespeople deemed imminent, an admirable effort to support his sales team, no doubt. But imagine his sense of frustration when it soon became apparent that his salespeople would not take the initiative to close any sales without him. Six months of a grueling pace found him physically exhausted while business in his district remained relatively unchanged.

This sales manager later admitted that he felt responsible for inadvertently sending out the wrong message to his sales staff. The message was that of the "Super Closer," and it dictated that he be involved in all potential closes.

"My sales organization reminded me of a basketball team that constantly hands off to the superstar. They were standing around and letting me do everything!" he complained.

When I asked him why he felt that he had found himself in this predicament, his response was classic. "I guess there are many reasons, but I truly believed that the reason I got promoted was because of my ability to close business. I assumed that was what management wanted from me as a manager. I didn't have faith in the abilities of my sales force, but I hoped that by watching me they would pick up the traits that had made me successful in the field."

Looking back, Bob admitted that he had failed in several ways. First, he had failed to define his job as a sales manager. Secondly, and more importantly, while he knew how to close, he didn't know how to train people. Thirdly, he didn't recognize that his managerial success was dependent on the success of his people. If they succeeded, he succeeded. If they failed, he failed. Doing it all himself didn't work. To achieve real success, Bob needed to multiply his talents by transferring the skills that had made him a successful salesman to his sales organization.

People can and do learn by example. But in order for this to happen, Bob would have to focus his salesperson's attention on the specific areas in the presentation where he or she might benefit from his techniques.

Bob: "When we see Mr. Brown today, let me try to close him. I want you to make special note of the way I get his concurrence at each step prior to asking for the order."

Previously, there had been no clear directions and, therefore, no way for Bob to be sure what his sales force was picking up from him. The misguided message must have been, "Cool it! The new manager likes to close the deals," rather than "The new manager wants us to learn how to close."

Fortunately, Bob recognized his error, re-evaluated his role, and went on to become the Vice President of Sales for a Fortune 100 company. But success for him came only after he put away the misguided belief that his primary role, as a manager, was that of a "Super Closer."

The Manager's Role in Closing

If the sales manager is not to be considered "Super Closer," what is his role in closing? How does he fit into this particular step in the sales process?

The sales manager has three important roles:

1. Training the sales organization.
2. Cementing customer/prospect relationships.
3. *Assisting* with the close of *difficult* sales.

Training the sales organization

Without a doubt, one of the sales manager's primary responsibilities is to guide, train, and support his salespeople.

But, as we have seen, this cannot be achieved by taking over in the field. Ideally, this work takes place before a sales call, in sales seminars, and at district/ branch meetings where the sales manager instructs his people in sales techniques and the preparation of account strategies. This effort is continued and reinforced constantly through regular sales call reviews following customer visits.

Cementing customer/prospect relationships

The sales manager's second role is to cement the relationship with a potential customer that his salesperson has begun to establish. All customers would like to feel that their orders are important, that they can pick up a phone and call someone who is not only familiar with their needs, but has the clout and authority to fix any problems that they run into quickly and effectively. Customers feel a certain added comfort knowing that a manager or, even better, a vice president, is in their corner.

That is why many successful companies have instituted ongoing executive visit programs. These programs are specifically designed to introduce and foster relationships between key executives on both sides of the sales table. Executive visit programs are an especially effective tool in signing and maintaining large, critical accounts.

Assisting with the close of difficult sales

Sometimes the sales manager must play a critical part in closing a sale. This is especially true if the salesperson lacks experience or closing skills, or in cases where the salesperson has had difficulty getting a commitment. However, even an experienced sales manager cannot close a sale unless his salesperson has done the preliminary work. If the groundwork has not been laid, the sales manager can bring few arguments to bear that will move the sale sufficiently along to close in one meeting. Sales managers who consider themselves "Super Closers" fool no one but themselves if they think they've done it alone.

The Sales Manager's True Role

The best way to define the sales manager's true role is to look at management's expectations. The easiest way to understand these expectations is to examine the characteristics they look for prior to promoting someone.

Is the salesperson who always exceeds his quota the one most likely to be promoted? Sometimes, but not always. Granted, management is unlikely to consider anyone for promotion who consistently fails to meet his quota. But given two candidates with good performance records, which one rises to the top in management's eyes?

There are three critical skills that are evaluated when management considers a person's promotability. Hence, these three skills effectively define much of the sales manager's role:

1. The ability to develop and manage people.
2. The ability to meet commitments.
3. The ability to see and solve problems.

The ability to develop and manage people

If polled, any executive worth his wide leather chair would list the ability to develop and manage people as his number one consideration when evaluating anyone for promotion. Where does the executive look to evaluate this skill? The executive need only look at the sales manager's people or to recall the conversations he has had with the manager about his people.

If the sales manager's organization is made up of aggressive superstars, you have a sure bet that the manager has provided the environment and training to develop his people to their fullest potential. If he bemoans his lot, if he is always claiming to be bogged down with weak, unmotivated salespeople, you can be just as sure he is failing to do his job. If he has no shining stars or is continually taking credit for all of the success of his organization, the executive has good reason to be wary.

This type of manager has failed to understand what the successful executive knows; that is, "If you haven't developed a successor, you are probably not promotable." That is not to say that, without a potential successor, you cannot get promoted, but a shining star, developed by you, can certainly make you look great! Your ability to move up the corporate ladder can be due, in part, to your ability to fill your own shoes. So be a forward-thinking manager. Work hard to train and develop your people. And remember that a large part of your job as a manager is to make your troops shine!

The ability to meet commitments

In any organization, at any level, meeting commitments and deadlines are important. This becomes even more critical as you move up in an organization. Superiors look to you for clear, complete, and timely reports on which they will base key decisions. Unfortunately, many salespeople are chronically lax when it comes to the timeliness and organization of their reports. These poor work habits often follow them when they become managers and grow in significance, unless a conscious effort is made to improve.

Years ago, I worked for a small start-up company where the salespeople reported directly to me. I reported directly to the president. I was required to prepare a monthly sales forecast that was based on what my individual salespeople submitted in their monthly reports. Their reports to me were due by the first of the month and, in turn, my forecast to the president was slated for the fifth. My top salesman, Dick, was chronically late. Many times, his report arrived after the fifth. When I reminded him of the necessity for timeliness, his usual excuse was that he was involved in some important sales situation that required his complete attention. He asked, "Do you want reports or sales?"

I knew that he spent a lot of time on the road, and I was sure that he was working hard. Even so, his tardiness rendered my forecasts to the president repeatedly incomplete. Naturally, the president questioned me, and I was forced to explain just what Dick was working on and to make excuses for him. It became downright embarrassing!

Dick was right to focus on sales. Nevertheless, I began to resent him for putting me in an awkward position with the president. His lack of responsiveness was not only rendering my forecasts inaccurate, but was reflecting on me as his manager. Finally, the president put it on the line. "If Dick can't do his job, get someone who can!"

Faced with that kind of ultimatum, Dick's performance in this area did improve. But his lack of responsibility in this area followed him and later surfaced as an issue when he was being considered for a management position. Despite his ability to bring in the sales, he was passed over when an opening in management occurred.

When I was working at AT&T a vice president requested specific information about various market segments from his department heads. While this information was available from many sources, the format he requested required considerable effort from all the staff. We did not believe that the information would render usable data, so most of us treated this request as a nuisance. Sixteen people were asked to respond. Only two department heads took the time to complete the assignment in a professional, timely manner. I will admit that I was not one of the two.

Those two respondents were the next to be promoted. Granted, I am sure the promotion decision was made for many reasons, the quality of their report and their timeliness being only part of the consideration, but I couldn't help but take notice. They had been able to distinguish themselves from their peers and had done so in a way that had drawn the attention of the vice president. Needless to say, I took the time to complete the next request and within the time requested. And who do you think was the next person promoted?

The ability to see and solve problems

The pressure to meet revenue objectives is a constant in the selling profession. Usually, a thousand and one problems stand in the way. Late product introductions, delivery delays, pricing concerns, competition; all present unique frustrations and challenges to the sales manager.

Effective, long-term resolutions of problems like these can sometimes be out of your hands. When this is the case, it is how you present yourself that will largely determine how you are perceived by management. Griping, grumbling, or complaining about things you cannot change will make you appear weak and immature.

If you cannot effect change, your only course of action is to present the problem concisely and professionally to management and then attempt to work, as best as you can, to minimize the impact of the problem on your organization until such time as solutions can be worked out by others.

It is unfortunate that many managers focus their energies on the problems, when they could be doing much to advance their reputations, even when they are somewhat hamstrung. One example immediately comes to mind. An order for 500 units could not be delivered in the two-week time frame that had been promised to one of my key customers. The sales manager was livid when he was informed of the manufacturing delay.

"How do you expect me to keep this customer when I can't get his initial order out on time?" he ranted. "I'll be darned if I'm gonna call my salesperson and tell him we can't ship the order for four weeks. Manufacturing had better get their act together or we'll end up losing all our credibility with this account!"

On and on, he went. I patiently listened while Dennis vented steam. When he was through, I directed him to call the customer, explain the problem, and determine how much product the customer really had to have in the initial shipment. Two hundred pieces were shipped in two weeks, with the remaining three hundred being sent two weeks later. The customer was happy, and the manufacturing department got its temporary reprieve. A simple phone call had provided the solution to what the sales manager considered an insurmountable problem.

In this case, the sales manager could not have been expected to solve manufacturing's production problem, but he did have an opportunity to demonstrate his problem-solving skills. Unfortunately, he didn't. He was too busy complaining.

Your ability to be a part of the solution, rather than an added burden to a problem has a major impact on your promotability. The presentation of problems and the ability to be perceived as a problem solver will be made more clear in upcoming chapters.

Other Factors Impacting Promotability

Fitting the mold

Management tends to promote people whose styles match their own. As much as we hate to admit it, it is a fact of life. Whether at work or in our personal lives, we have a tendency to surround ourselves with people who share our ideas and with whom we feel comfortable. Therefore, given two candidates with similar backgrounds, the one that best fits with the corporate culture will usually get the nod for that next promotion.

However, in the business arena most companies can and will overlook a mismatch, if you are an outstanding performer. John DeLorean is an example of someone who made his way up through the ranks of General Motors despite his unique and unorthodox style. If you feel that you are somewhat of a maverick and have been bypassed for promotion because of your style, it may be time to step back and make an honest assessment of your work and your personal style as it relates to your work. If you really want to get a handle on your performance, ask your boss or his boss.

Your lead-in could be:

> "Scott, I need your help. I've noticed that Judy and Don have been promoted recently. I believe they are good choices, but I would like to know what you feel I have to do to be considered promotable."

If you do this, be prepared to listen. Do not try to rationalize your actions or win debating points. Your purpose is to gather information, and while you may win points, you run the risk of losing the opportunity to advance.

If you leave this meeting still believing that your stagnation is a direct result of your maverick ways, you have only three choices:

- To continue as before, fully realizing that, barring some radical change in management, the perception of your style will make your chances for promotion slim.
- To attempt to make some compromises or changes that will allow you to fit in with the existing culture.
- To look for another job.

Your political instincts

Most of us dislike "playing politics," but feel sure that it's the only way to get ahead. Right? Wrong! One would be naive to think that "who you know and how you know them" doesn't enter into the decision process in many companies. The extent to which politics plays a part in promotions varies from company to company, but I truly believe that this factor has been drastically overrated. In most promotions, performance, not politics, is the key factor. Look around and check out who is being promoted in your own company. Is it only the people who have the corporate ear? Or are there people being promoted from out in the field, people who have little access to those making the promotion decisions? If you've been passed over for promotion and are convinced that your inability to play the political game is the reason, I strongly suggest that you re-evaluate your performance. Again, I suggest that you start by talking to your boss or his boss.

If you do find that your performance has not been the critical hang-up, you might want to consider that you have merely failed to position your accomplishments in the best light possible.

Positioning your accomplishments

Do you believe that your boss knows all the great things that you have accomplished? Do you believe he knows and truly understands the effort and time you exerted to develop the brilliant strategy that won the ABC contract? Whether he does or doesn't depends on how frequently you talk to him and how you describe your activities. In most cases, conversations between sales managers and their bosses are brief. They focus on pressing issues, revenue objectives, how the month is proceeding, and general overviews. You may not have the time to articulate the brilliant strategy that helped you land the ABC contract and you cannot assume that he knows. Nor can you assume that he knows about the innovative technique you used to improve Bill's performance or how well you handled the conflict between the technical support people and Sandy last week. So, how do you position your accomplishments without looking like you are breaking your arm patting yourself on the back?

I suggest setting up a meeting with your boss and his, if possible, once every six months. The objective is to review your activities over the previous six months and your plans for the following six months. A recommended format for the meeting would be similar to the one discussed in Chapter 20, "Senior Sales Managements Visits," with the addition of a discussion of your most recent accomplishments.

Bring your boss up-to-date on any outstanding "wins" you've had in the last few months. You should emphasize the specific strategy your organization employed, including all the specific steps that were taken to land the customer. This format will also provide you with an opportunity to position accomplishments unrelated to specific customers (staff issues, training programs, etc.).

Here is one more important suggestion. Avoid using the word I. Use the word "we." This will reinforce your image as a team player. Keep your conversation low key. Don't brag. In other words, toot your horn, but don't make it reveille!

BASIC PRINCIPLES

As sales manager your job is to:

- Develop and manage people
- Meet commitments
- Solve problems

Your role in closing is to:

- Train your sales organization in all aspects of the selling process
- Cement customer/prospect relationships
- Assist with the close of difficult sales

15

INHERITING AN EXISTING ORGANIZATION

Most managers who get promoted or are moved into a new territory want to make an immediate impact to prove to their management that they are decisive and worthy of their new position. Oftentimes, this activity takes the form of a quick realignment of the district or organization. In general, this kind of "shoot-from-the-hip" management backfires. It unnerves the rank and file, puts people on the defensive, and builds immediate distrust and resentment. How many times have you heard a fellow employee grumble, "He's got nerve marching in here like he knows it all. He's barely stepped foot in the place, and he's got all the answers already!" Take advantage of the "honeymoon" period that follows a promotion or change. Step back and take a good hard look at what you've inherited. Do absolutely nothing in terms of changing things until you have completed the following:

- A territory review
- Flushed out the key issues, concerns, and inhibitors to success
- Participated in sales calls with each member of your team
- Listened to and understood the needs of your team

What you want to do is build on the success of your organization and be fully aware of all the implications of your plans before you make any moves. Yes! I said "Build on the success of your organization!" No matter how poor an organization appears, there are things being done correctly. Come in with guns blazing and you'll wipe out your chances for finding your organization's strengths.

Ted E. was recently appointed General Manager of a small division of a large and diverse company in the Midwest. Recognizing that he had inherited difficult revenue objectives from his predecessor and wanting to make a quick impact, he embarked on a superficial review of his organization. After spending no more than one-and-a-half hours with each key member of his team, he made significant organizational changes. A year later, his previously profitable division showed substantial losses.

Ted had not taken the time to assess fully the ability and capabilities of his people prior to making his organizational changes. Following his recommendations, key personnel were moved around and placed in new positions. In some cases, people found themselves in positions they were not qualified to handle, resulting in a loss of marketing, advertising, and product focus. Engineering project dates slipped, and the products that did manage to emerge lacked the clear marketing launch plans necessary to make them successful.

It is important to realize that companies, organizations, and groups have formal and informal procedures that are not immediately apparent to new personnel. Making changes too quickly can disrupt the informal working relationships within an organization and with customers. Prior to Ted's arrival, a group of three people, who reported to the sales division, handled technical support issues. This small group was highly competent and technically skilled. Their primary formal responsibility was customer training, but over time they added several informal duties that did not appear on the organization charts or in their job descriptions. These duties included responding to technical product problems, complaint follow-up, and the preparation of major proposals. They were the single point of contact for handling customer complaints and technical problems and understood how to work through the organization to resolve a myriad of customer concerns.

During the reorganization all three were moved to the marketing department and assigned new responsibilities. As customer problems arose, salespeople had no place to go for answers. No one organization had complete responsibility for handling customer problems. It took several weeks to develop a new system for handling this key responsibility. In the interim, several customers lost faith in the company's ability to respond in a timely manner. Ted had effectively eliminated the single point of contact that so many customers preferred.

If you don't understand the system completely, leave it alone until you do!

The Territory Review

Your initial territory review can be considered a "get acquainted" session with your staff. It can be held with the entire group or individually. Your primary focus at this point should be on evaluating your salespeople relative to meeting their revenue objectives. But you are not in a position to evaluate fully what you are told until you have become better acquainted with your entire staff and are more familiar with their territories.

There are two different approaches one can take prior to meeting with your new team. The approach you choose will depend on your management style and what you are attempting to evaluate.

The first approach is to send out a rather general letter stating your intention to meet with your salespeople and informing them that you would like them to be prepared to give a brief sales review at this meeting. This general letter leaves the presentation and format of the sales review up to the salesperson. The obvious advantage to this approach is that it gives you a good indication of how well organized the salesperson is and how he responds when faced with minimal direction. You will also get a good indication of whether he generally presents himself in a logical and orderly fashion or not. The disadvantage is that, in giving a free hand, the salesperson may not address all the topics or cover all the information you may have wanted to discuss. Be sure to inform your salesperson of the time limitations so he can plan accordingly.

The second method is to request the presentation of specific information. This makes the initial meeting more efficient and will give you a better understanding of the revenue potential in a given territory. Even though you will be able to gain some insight into your salesperson, you will not be able to garner as much about him personally as you would with the first approach.

If you use this second method, the format for a Territory Plan, as suggested in Chapter 2, may assist you in formulating basic guidelines for this first "get acquainted" review.

Remember, this review is your opportunity to position yourself as a manager who wants to help his people and gain their loyalty and trust. It is not the time to criticize. Instead, ask questions and listen. You want your sales force open and comfortable enough to share their honest concerns.

You can choose any number of ways to elicit the information you want without sounding critical or dictatorial. Whatever you do, NEVER USE THE WORDS "WHY DIDN'T YOU" or "YOU SHOULD HAVE"! Statements that begin with "Why didn't you" and "You should have" make the salesperson defensive and can close communication quickly. The salesperson is put into the position of having to defend his actions rather than sharing them with you.

A better approach might go like this:

> "Not knowing enough about this account, would it make
> sense to approach the customer by reiterating the finan-
> cial benefits in this package?

> "How were the financial benefits presented to the presi-
> dent?"

> "You mentioned meeting with some resistance from the
> financial vice president. How did you handle that?"

In each case, a question is asked. I am not dictating an
approach or drawing attention to an error. In the first example, a particular approach is suggested but phrased in such
a way that the salesperson need not feel threatened. He is free
to accept the suggestion or tell why it has not worked for him
in the past.

The Manager as a Problem Solver

During this initial review, you should give each salesperson an opportunity to articulate his customers' complaints.
It is important for your salespeople to understand that the
purpose will be to search for solutions and find courses of
action that will eliminate the complaints.

I have always told my staff, "If you have a problem that
may affect the sale, I want to hear about it. After you've lost
the sale, don't come to me using problems that weren't
brought to my attention as excuses. At that point, I don't want
to hear that John in Engineering didn't answer your questions
or that samples to the customers didn't arrive in time. If you
lost the sale as a result of someone in the company not
responding, but didn't let me know about it, you are the one

that is accountable. But if you tell me about it, it is up to me to get you what you need or to fix the problem. If I can't help you, we will review alternative strategies to try and satisfy the customer's requests."

Many problems are not directly related to closing sales but act as irritants to the salesperson, taking attention away from the selling function. These issues may take any number of forms, from a salesperson's frustration with the payroll department for failing to issue his commission check on time or accurately, to his need for a PC or fax machine to make him more efficient. If you are unsure when confronted with these problems, tell your staff that you are not sure what can be done, but assure them that you will look into their concerns. Make sure you do. Do not make any promises lightly, as employee frustration only intensifies if you are not good to your word and fail to follow through. Get into the habit of sending a letter with your responses to their concerns as quickly after your discussion as possible.

Other Personnel

Don't overlook the rest of your organization either. Spend time with each member of your organization. Ask them to:

- Describe their job
- Identify what they like about it
- Identify what they dislike about it
- Identify the types of problems they run across that make it difficult for them to perform their jobs satisfactorily
- State their key issues and concerns

Just as you did with your salespeople, you want to try and resolve any issues and concerns that could impact performance. Personnel should know that they can bring problems to you that they are unable to resolve on their own.

BASIC PRINCIPLES

Make NO changes until you have:

- Completed a territory review.

- Flushed out the key issues, concerns, and inhibitors to success.

- Participated in sales calls with each member of your team.

- Listen to and understand the needs of your team.

Position yourself as a problem solver. Eliminate the roadblocks that interfere with your salespeople's ability to make their sales quotas.

16

PROFESSIONAL COACHING

"Brains, like hearts, go where they are appreciated."
Robert McNamara

There are three primary goals in coaching:

- To REINFORCE good performance
- To IMPROVE unsatisfactory performance
- To MAINTAIN and IMPROVE motivation

It is a shame that many managers feel that the only way to change the performance of their organization is by taking dictatorial and threatening postures. Screaming, threatening, and insulting your staff shows your loss of control. Humiliating and berating your people only serves to instill animosity and fear. Neither accomplishes long-term change. If you expect professional attitudes from your people, you must act in a professional manner yourself. To earn respect, you must show respect.

I thought long and hard before settling on a title for this chapter. For me, the term "coaching" invokes an image of someone I would have confidence in; someone who would urge me on and encourage me to perform at my best.

Hopefully, if you accept your role as that of a coach, not a tyrant or overlord, your people will soon recognize that your intention is to develop their natural talents and skills.

They will accept your instruction as something worthwhile and in their best interest.

So, without further comment, let's look at the role of the sales manager as coach.

THE FIVE KEY ELEMENTS
OF PROFESSIONAL COACHING

Let's examine the five key elements needed to modify your sales staff's performance while still maintaining mutual respect and morale.

1. Review the sales call immediately after the field visit.
2. Get feedback from the salesperson first.
3. Always start with a compliment.
4. Gain concurrence on the areas needing improvement as well as the time frames involved.
5. Document your conversation.

Review the sales call immediately after the field visit

Like the coach who huddles in the locker room following a game, it is important for you to review the sales call as soon as possible after the customer visit. A review days after the visit may not be of much value to your salesperson. Conversations and actions become hazy over time. However, a lag in time would still be preferable to trying to review anything with your salesperson while running for a plane or racing for the next sales call. It is up to you to plan sufficient time to discuss and critique the call. It is imperative that you have the salesperson's attention. It needn't be a formal conference, but could be done while having lunch, dinner, or a cup of coffee in a quiet place without distractions.

Get feedback from your salesperson first

Before reviewing any aspects of the call, ask the sales-person what he thought about the visit. This provides him with the opportunity to share his perspective on his perfor-mance. You'd be surprised how many times I've asked for and received a pretty honest assessment of my salesperson's performance. Many will say, "I was not happy with the way I handled _____," or, "I believe I should have pushed harder for _____."

The salespeople who recognize their mistakes tend to be the better performers. Often a salesperson will point out areas of his performance that are troubling him, areas you might have missed. This self-recognition is the first step toward improvement. When the salesperson critiques him-self, you are in a position to act as his coach. He is looking for your assistance. More importantly, he is open to your suggestions.

The salesperson's own performance review can give you new insights into why he approached things as he did. Often, I have suggested an alternate strategy, only to have my salesperson mention that he had tried the same approach in a previous visit.

"I realize that you feel that I should have pushed harder for the order, but let me tell you what happened the last time."

This feedback will give you a better perspective and will give you time to think about what you want to cover.

Always start with a compliment

If you learn nothing else from this chapter, always start with a compliment. However minor the accomplishment, see it and recognize it. If a person recognizes that good perfor-mance will be praised, you are guaranteed that he will try his hardest to earn more of it in the future. That is human nature!

Starting with the positive will also put your salesperson at ease and set a positive environment that is conducive to introducing areas needing improvement.

Everyone knows how to compliment. Right? Wrong! Let's take a brief moment to look at what constitutes a good compliment. First of all, BE SPECIFIC!

"Keep up the good work," or "You're doing a good job," is not specific.

"Susan, you qualified your prospect well. Three times the prospect said he was not interested in buying the product. But you were persistent. I like that! Every time he voiced an objection, you were able to get at the heart of his concern and come back with a reply that turned the situation around."

That was specific! If you expect to see the behavior again, you must compliment it specifically.

In the same vein, always emphasize behavior. Saying something like "the customers seem to like you" is vague and focuses on reactions to behavior, not the behavior itself. In fact, such statements may reinforce undesirable behavior. Does the salesperson think he's popular because he tells jokes?

Something like, "I sense that the customers appreciate that whenever there is a problem, you are always willing to pitch in and spend the time necessary to see that it is corrected," is much more precise.

Be consistent and be honest in your praise. Praise only what is deserved; I am not advocating insincerity here. It has been my experience that you can find something praiseworthy in most situations, if you are looking for it. But if you cannot see it, you would be better served by not saying anything at all. People can sense insincerity and it is never respected.

Finally, be proportionate in your praise. The amount of praise lavished on someone should be proportionate to what they have accomplished and the difficulty of the task. Don't be a gusher. That rings just as untrue as the insincere compliment and can be as counterproductive.

Gain concurrence on the areas needing improvement, as well as the time frames involved

One of the most common mistakes made by sales managers occurs when they fail to get closure or agreement on the areas they have earmarked for change or improvement. An open-ended review with a salesperson renders little in the way of long-term change and is quickly forgotten. It is important to clarify and document what has been agreed upon and stipulate target dates for any changes that are to be made. A simple summary of what was covered and agreed upon might go something like this:

> "John, we covered a lot of ground today. Let's recap the key items that we're going to focus on in the next several weeks. As we discussed, the number of face-to-face visits is low. I'd like to see them increased from an average of four per day to six. Let's try to achieve this objective over the next two weeks. Does that sound like a reasonable goal to you?"

If John had said that two weeks was not reasonable, suggesting more like three or four, I would not have argued. John's agreement and "buy in" are the crucial factors here. However, if John had said five visits instead of six, I might have pointed out that six was the norm and what I expected. Obviously, each case requires that you make judgement calls about what you are willing and unwilling to negotiate.

The more specific you are, the more likely you are to get the results you seek. Be as clear about your expectations as possible.

"As we discussed, it is important to gather information about the company prior to your sales presentation. We discussed how this might be accomplished and how it can help you. I'd like you to focus on getting the following information:
- Information regarding the size of the company, their products, customers etc.
- Identify the customer's business problem
- Identify the key decision makers and influencers
- Determine their decision cycle

Do you anticipate any problems with this?"

The Case for Specificity

Four months after Lynn was promoted to district manager, her vice president expressed disappointment in the way she was managing her territory. Lynn naturally asked her boss to be more specific.

"I thought you would have taken action on Bill by now."

"What action did you want me to take?" Lynn asked, confused.

"I told you I didn't think he could close business, and I would have thought, by this time, you would have fired him."

Lynn was flabbergasted. The vice president had never told her that this was his expectation.

"How could he hold me accountable for something he never told me? I thought he wanted me to work with Bill, to bring him up to speed," she later told me.

Clearly, the vice president had not communicated his expectations. Is it any surprise that he had not seen the results he had expected? He should have said, "Lynn, I am not happy with Bill's performance. I don't believe that he can close business. I want you to evaluate him. If you feel that he has the potential to improve, I want to see a plan that will bring him around within another three months. Otherwise, I want you to fire him by the end of the quarter."

Document the Results

After getting concurrence, follow-up is critical. You should send a letter reiterating what was agreed upon as soon as possible after every visit. There are several reasons for this. First, it emphasizes that you consider the visit and the review important. Hence, the smart salesperson realizes that he must consider it important too. Secondly, it reminds him of his commitment and eliminates any misunderstandings as to what was said and agreed upon.

The letter also serves as the basis for subsequent measurement of improvement. It is the salesperson's tangible evidence of growth and progress and an invaluable reference for managers when preparing yearly performance reviews.

Lastly, it can be a safeguard in the event that disciplinary action must later be taken. I cannot count the number of times subordinates have come to me, unhappy with the performance of one of their people, and seeking permission to let the employee go. Invariably, I ask them if they have informed the employee of their dissatisfaction. The answer is usually an unequivocal yes. But when asked to produce the documentation of those conversations, these same people grow suddenly silent. Documentation for these purposes may be distasteful, but it is also necessary.

In many large companies, there is a three to six month process one must go through prior to firing any employee. This process requires detailed documentation to prove that the employee was informed of his superior's dissatisfaction and given a fair chance to improve his performance. Needless to say, failure to keep records of conversations not only puts one in a legal bind, but greatly delays the dismissal process.

SAMPLE EVALUATION LETTER

Dear John:

This is to summarize our discussion regarding the sales visits we made last week.

As I told you, I was very pleased with your presentation. You have an excellent understanding of our product features and a good technical background.

As we discussed, there are several areas I would like you to work on that will improve your sales performance. Success in these areas should aid you in meeting your revenue objectives.

Prior to beginning your presentation, it is important to ask questions so that you can find out as much about the company as you can, specifically:

The customer's business problem
The names of the key decision makers/influencers
Their decision cycle
The size of the company, their products etc.

This information is vital in order to position the benefits our product can bring to the customer and how they can solve his business problem. As I mentioned, product features are only important as they relate to user benefits.

On your future visits, you should focus on finding out and documenting this information. I will evaluate your progress in this area on my next visit.

I hope to get back to Phoenix sometime in September and will look forward to doing the rounds with you again.

Sincerely,

Employee Evaluations

As a manager, you have a responsibility to attempt to improve the performance of your subordinates. Most companies require that each employee be reviewed every six to twelve months. Yet, most managers feel inadequate and uncomfortable with this responsibility, especially if an evaluation requires the discussion of weak areas. Few of us feel comfortable drawing attention to another's shortcomings, so the technique of starting with the person's strengths is a good one to use here also.

I know! I know! You wish you could stop there, right? But only identifying strengths won't help this person improve. Perhaps it would be helpful to think of yourself as that coach again. As coach, your job is to get your salesperson down that field and within reach of his goal. From the sidelines, you can see the goal quite clearly, but you also see all the things that are standing between your salesperson and that goal. It's up to you to help him overcome or maneuver around the obstacles that could stop him.

When I was at AT&T, my first performance review was one that I'll never forget. My manager was a great guy named Jack. I respected and admired him, so you can imagine my embarrassment when he tactfully pointed out my tendency to cut people off when they were talking. I remember turning to him and saying, "If anybody else had told me this, I don't know whether I would have believed them." But I trusted Jack. I knew he was looking down the field, so to speak. I knew the topic was uncomfortable for him. He would only bring it up if he truly believed that it was going to stand in my way down the line. Was I embarrassed? You bet! Did I ignore it? No way! I made a point of trying to eliminate that habit and went on to be promoted.

A long time has gone by since then, but I often think about that review. I seriously doubt if I would have been promoted if Jack didn't have the backbone to meet his responsibility that day. I have always admired him for being honest and calling it like he saw it, despite the discomfort.

BASIC PRINCIPLES

The three primary goals in coaching are:

- To REINFORCE good performance

- To IMPROVE unsatisfactory performance

- To MAINTAIN and IMPROVE motivation

The five key elements of professional coaching are:

- Review the sales call immediately after the field visit

- Get feedback from the salesperson before you begin to speak

- Always start with a compliment

- Gain concurrence on the areas needing improvement, as well as the time frames involved

- Document your conversation

17

CONDUCTING TERRITORY REVIEWS

A territory review should be a detailed discussion between a manager and a salesperson at which time agreement is reached regarding the way revenue objectives will be achieved. The outcome should render concrete activities that will ensure that revenue objectives will be reached, with dates that can be tracked.

Unfortunately, many managers use the territory review as an opportunity to "beat up" their sales force. I once knew an executive vice president who only called in his sales organization for updates when sales were running below forecast. Before the first salesperson was five minutes into his presentation, Ed would start his badgering.

"What is this garbage? You forecasted a close on that account this month! I don't want to hear any excuses. I want it closed in the next thirty days!" he would scream.

"You are 80 percent of forecast. If you know what's good for you, you'd better be up to forecast in 60 days!"

"You forecasted closing Company A in 90 days. Get on the stick. I want that customer closed in 45 days!"

This kind of berating would continue throughout the presentations. Other than terrorizing his sales organization, Ed's reviews rarely accomplished anything. If sales failed to improve, the brutalized sales force would be called in for yet another browbeating. Turnover in the company was extremely high. Of the twenty-two salespeople who were hired in one three month period, only two were still working at the company two years later. To survive, salespeople had to develop thick skins or learn to ignore Ed's outbursts.

If a territory review is not to be used as a steam vent for management, it should not be viewed as just another broad-brush update on account and territory status either. Too often, territory reviews turn into meaningless monologues where salespeople talk in general and often glowing terms about their potential closes, and managers politely and passively listen. Obviously, when this happens, managers leave with "warm fuzzies" but carry away no concrete information on which they can assess the progress of the plans they have heard. In these situations, salespeople soon learn to give impressive, but shallow, presentations, knowing that they can put their plans back on the shelf as soon as the manager leaves.

These reviews are characterized by their vagueness:

N.Y. Tel is holding its own. At this point last year, we were looking at about $500,000 in revenue. We're running a little ahead of that level this year. The N. Y. Tel. contract comes up for renewal in three months. As you know, our major competitor is AT&T. We're maintaining 70 - 80 percent of the business that's generated and see no reason to anticipate any changes in that percentage. They also have a major job coming up in their upstate branch. I think you can rest assured that we'll land our share of that contract.

The manager who accepts this kind of presentation walks away feeling quite satisfied that everything has been covered with the account, even though he has not received a single piece of information to indicate how his salesperson plans to achieve the anticipated results.

An experienced and competent sales manager would never accept this kind of vague, overly confident, presentation. If N. Y. Telephone was an important account, at the very least, he would have asked to see a prepared KAAP that detailed the activities that were planned. In the absence of such a plan, the manager's immediate reaction should be to question the salesperson further.

> I appreciate your confidence, Joe. Can you be more specific about your plans over the next three months and how you think that they will ensure that we will get the business? Who are the key decision makers and influencers and how do you plan to cover them? What do you plan to tell them?

The responsible sales manager would continue to question and draw out the information he needed to assist Joe in formulating specific plans to guarantee that all the bases were covered with the account.

To ensure that your salespeople's territory plans are well defined and complete, you should ask the following questions before you close any territory review:

- Does this salesperson have specific account plans in place for all key accounts? Have those plans been defined in detail? That is, what is going to be done, by whom and when?

- Does this salesperson recognize the role of key decision makers and influencers? Does he have a plan in place to address their chief concerns?

- Have the major business problems/"hot buttons" been defined?

- Are there plans in place to address the small- and medium-sized customers?

- Have plans been developed for the introduction of new products?

- Have we agreed on time frames for each of his activities?

- Do I have enough information to track all the activities, dates, and outcomes?

A territory review should be conducted, at least semiannually, with each of your salespeople. The meeting should be an interchange of ideas between you and your salesperson where the best plan for reaching the revenue objectives is developed. Your role should be one of trying to determine that all the aspects of a particular situation have been covered and reviewed.

BASIC PRINCIPLES

A territory review should be an interchange of ideas between you and your salesperson where the best plan for reaching the revenue objectives is agreed upon.

A territory review should not be used as an opportunity to "beat up" on your sales organization.

18
THE GREAT TEMPTATION: OVERCOMMITMENT

At the end of the year, the board of directors looks to the president for an explanation of why he failed to meet his revenue commitment. The president then looks to the Vice President of Sales for an explanation of why he failed to meet his revenue commitment. The Vice President of Sales looks to his sales manager for an explanation of why he failed to meet his revenue commitment. At the end of the year, the sales manager looks skyward and says, "Why?"

There are many reasons for revenue shortfalls, but there is one reason that is so common, so basic, and so fundamental as to be often overlooked. What all of these professionals have failed to consider or understand is the impact that "lead-times" have on forecasted revenue. Companies readily incorporate and accept "lead-times" for R&D projects, but even savvy sales managers fail to consider "lead-times" as they apply to sales.

Let's look at two examples. One a corporate perspective, the other an overly optimistic sales manager's chronic dilemma.

The Corporate Perspective

At the June management meeting, top management declares that it is their desire to increase sales by five million dollars the next year. As manager, you wonder how they pulled that particular number out of the hat? But you can't wonder about it too long, because the clock is ticking, and you've got to figure out some way to perform this miracle.

There are three ways you can increase sales. The first is to increase sales productivity through training or the introduction of new products. Another is to hire more salespeople to obtain better coverage of the territories. A third would be to look at a combination of these approaches.

Management often fails to consider that there comes a time when you cannot increase the revenue generated per salesperson any further. They may accept this limit on productivity from other divisions from within the company, but tend to ignore or not understand this principle when considering sales. In too many companies management establishes sales goals without any detailed planning on how to achieve those goals. Their underlying assumption seems to be that the existing sales organization "can do it," or that the products are so marvelous as to sell themselves.

The sales manager should remember that, depending on several factors such as territory size, average revenue per sale, sales cycles etc., a salesperson reaches a revenue plateau.

But for the sake of argument, let's say that you have taken that into account, and figure that, with training, you can safely raise sales productivity from 1.25 million per salesperson to 1.5 million.

Given an organization of ten salespeople, you believe you can secure 2.5 million of the 5 million for which you are being held accountable. That still leaves you with a 2.5 million dollar shortfall. The only way you're going to make it is with new hires.

Let's examine what happens once you realize this. You tell management that in order to make the revenue forecast for next year, you need to hire two more salespeople. If they grant this request, the assumption is that each new salesperson will have a revenue objective of 1.5 million dollars for the following year. They approve your request within the month.

Let's assume, that from the time you put in your hiring request (July) to the day you have your salespeople "on board," is three months. This is a reasonable assumption. Another month passes as your new hires complete their product training and become familiar with their territories. Let's further assume that the average sell cycle for your products is six months; sell cycle being defined as the time that elapses from the first customer contact to the day that an actual order is placed.

Your new salespeople start pounding the pavement and bring in their first orders on schedule in May, ten months from the date they were hired. But delivery time, the time that elapses from the receipt of the order to the delivery of the product, which is when the revenue is booked, is an additional two months. From the date of your hiring request to the delivery of the product for the first sales is a full twelve months. If the salespeople meet their quota in the period from July 1st to December 31, they will sell $750,000 worth of product. In this hypothetical situation, your two new salespeople will show total sales of only $1,500,000 for the year. You will have a revenue shortfall of 1.0 million dollars.

In the event that an existing territory is split between an established salesperson and a new one, this same principle applies. The new salesperson can count on some revenue from existing business, but the salesperson who relinquished his accounts has to start from scratch developing new accounts to make up for the loss. In effect this situation is not unlike the one for the new salesperson in a new undeveloped territory. Revenue still has to be garnered from new accounts with the same lead times in either case. The situation is made even worse in those companies with long product selling cycles who do not set their revenue objectives for the new year until September.

The only way this hypothetical company could have met its objective is if they began the recruiting process six months earlier, in January. This would require that the company develop a realistic two- to three-year revenue plan. Many companies don't do this for several reasons. First, they don't understand the principles we have just discussed. Secondly, they don't want to take on the financial burden of new salespeople unless and until they have to. Companies often accept the hiring and paying of engineers to develop products that may be months if not years away but won't hire salespeople in the same manner. Thirdly, they do not take the planning function seriously and do not consider plans as working documents. In general, American companies view planning as an exercise required by the company or the board of directors. After completing these required plans, they are relegated to the shelf where they may not be looked at until the next planning cycle, which is a year off.

Do you now understand why the conversation at the beginning of this chapter occurs over and over in thousands of companies every year?

The Optimistic Sales Manager

Let's look at a somewhat different situation. You tell your management that you can increase revenue by one million dollars if they authorize the hiring of one additional salesperson. On January 2, you receive that authorization and, like it or not, the burden of your revenue commitment comes with it.

Upper management's perception is that since you have the requisition on January 2, you should be able to make your new committed revenue objective within twelve months. That perception is, of course, based on your promise to increase revenue by one million dollars if, and when, they allow you to hire the additional person, right?

As in the previous example, a full twelve months passes from the date of approved requisition to the delivery of that additional person's sold product. The additional revenue you would actually see for the year is definitely not one million dollars. In this hypothetical, but realistic example, you would not see any revenue in this calendar year at all. Even if your new salesperson did manage to bring in revenue earlier than anticipated, he/she would still fall far short of your one million dollar forecast.

You'd be in major trouble! The lesson to be learned is simple: figure lead times when making a revenue commitment and clearly state your assumptions when presenting revenue forecasts.

BASIC PRINCIPLES

Figure lead times when making any revenue commitment.

19

HIRING/INTERVIEWING

Your success as a sales manager will depend on the success of your people. Given that it takes three to six months for a new salesperson to become fully effective, and it probably takes that long to terminate a nonperformer, the selection process is critical.

Recruiting

Shawn, a recruiter, was following up on the interviews of several candidates with his client. All the candidates had been flown to Chicago from Dallas at the client's expense. When asked about the interviews, the client responded that none of the candidates had been suitable. Upon further questioning, the client indicated that none of the candidates had industry knowledge. The client was quite adamant that this qualification was even more important than a strong technical background. Shawn reviewed the job description supplied to him. In big, bold letters it stated that a strong technical background was mandatory, but made no mention of any need for specific industry knowledge. The out-of-pocket costs incurred by his client, which included airfare and other expenses, totaled $2,500.

I've talked to many recruiters, and they all have told me that a good job description allows the recruiting firm to quickly identify qualified candidates, thereby reducing the time that the client must spend on interviews.

155

One successful recruiter who specializes in placing officer-level candidates with start-up companies told me about one of his early frustrations with placements. He had been assigned the job of finding a president for a high tech company. Every candidate he recommended for the position was rejected. He sat back to analyze the problem and realized that the candidates were being interviewed, not only by the board of directors that had prepared the job description, but by the personnel who would be reporting to the president as well. These people had not been consulted when the job description had been prepared. The qualities they felt were necessary for the candidate differed markedly from those of the board. Their negative feedback following the interviews was reflecting this disparity.

This same recruiter now routinely develops the job description for his clients. Given the same situation, he now interviews not only the members of the board, but the personnel that will be reporting to the president as well. If there are major discrepancies between these parties, he knows he will not be successful until he reconciles their different requirements.

The same problem occurs in many companies when potential sales candidates are interviewed by several people from different organizations. Each interviewer has his own perception of the type of characteristics he would like to see in a candidate. Someone from an engineering background may look for strong technical skills, while another team member may not consider this critical at all. To be successful, it is imperative that all interviewers be made aware of what is and is not important. One will usually continue to get mixed reviews and fail to get closure unless the individuals conducting the interviews understand what is being sought. Thus, a good, clear job description not only gives recruiters an understanding of the type of individual a company is looking for, but also clarifies the qualifications for those within the company.

As sales manager, you should oversee the preparation of job descriptions for your organization and make sure that each of the key players has a copy of that job description prior to any interviews. Do not abdicate this responsibility. It is up to you to approve the description. The countless hours that could be wasted in fruitless interviewing will more than offset the small amount of time needed to develop a clear description. Remember that the revenue shortfall resulting from an open, unattended territory reflects on you, so take the time to do it well.

Development of the Job Description

Answers to the following questions will help you in preparing your job description:

I. Characteristics of my successful people

A. What are the characteristics of my best sales-people and what makes them successful?
1. Technical background?
2. Experience?
3. Industry knowledge?
4. Systems selling?
5. Good prospecting skills?
6. Software expertise?
7. Financial analysis skills?
8. Problem solving strengths?
9. Listening skills?
10. Presentation skills?

B. Identify discernible pattern

II. What are the specific skills needed to sell new/ anticipated products/markets?

Many times the answers to this question are the same as those of A. However, as companies develop new products and/or sell into new markets, they may find that the skills required to sell these new products/markets are different than those that were required before.

In the 1980s, the Teletype Corporation sold commodity-type products through original equipment manufacturers and distributors.[15] Under development was a series of systems-oriented products. System products typically have longer sell cycles, and the product features, as they relate to solving the customer's business problems, are critical. In Teletype's case, the new products were to be sold directly to the end user, had sell cycles of six to nine months, and required a sales organization that had the ability to sell customer benefits.

Teletype was successful in the sale of this next generation of products because they immediately recognized the need to:

- Retrain existing sales personnel and move those who could not adapt to the new environment into different positions.
- Hire new people who understood how to sell systems products.
- Develop faster service response which would be required by the customers purchasing these products

Many companies have failed in introducing new products and selling to new markets because they have not recognized and planned for the new skills required to sell, service, and support these products/markets.

---

[15]Commodity products are those products where features cannot be differentiated, that is, the product features are the same from company to company. Companies selling commodity products sell predominantly based on price.

III. Who will the salesperson's customers be?

Engineers?
Consumers?
Purchasing Agents?
Manufacturing/Shop Personnel?
Financial Personnel?
Corporate Level Presidents, Vice Presidents, and Department Heads?

It's amazing how much clearer your candidate will become as you consider these key contacts.

IV. Corporate culture—team makeup

What are the characteristics you consider to be important to your candidate's success within the company? If the company has a strong technical bent, someone weak in this area will not be well received. If the company tends to be "laid-back," an intense, hard-driving candidate will unsettle everyone. If professionalism is important, your candidate had better be the same. Is your company team-oriented or does it reward individualists? Occasionally, this exercise will flush out a characteristic that is dictated by the corporate culture, but not mandated by the market you serve.

Based on these lists, you now need to prioritize the skills you isolated. These skills should be grouped in the following categories:

- "Must Have"—The candidate MUST possess these to be considered.
- "Important" —The candidate should possess 80 percent of the skills listed in this category.
- "Nice to Have"—These skills may be disregarded, or, in the event that two candidates have equal credentials, help to "tip the scales."

The Interview Process

Now you've done your homework and a potential candidate nervously sits before you. How do you garner the information you need to see if there is a match?

Showstoppers

During the interview process, two things stand out in my mind as immediate "showstoppers." The first is a candidate's constant use of the word "I." It has been my experience that this may indicate that a candidate is not a team player. This type of individual may not recognize the importance that other members of an organization play in the sales process. When an individual is "I" focused rather than "We" focused, he may run into resistance from other members of the company and fail to get the cooperation and support he needs in so many sales situations. Granted, a candidate may be trying to impress you, underplaying the role that others played in his previous successes, but it pays to investigate this further. You might want to probe with questions like:

> "Did any other members of your team participate in this sale?"
> "If so, what did they contribute to the sales process?"
> "Did you consider any other coworkers instrumental in landing this sale?"
> "How did they assist you?"

If the candidate downplays anyone else's participation, you might want to steer clear.

The second thing that sends up red flags in an interview occurs if a candidate gives you information that does not sound reasonable. As an example, let's assume that the product that the candidate is selling has a six-month sell cycle.

The territory quota is one million dollars. If the candidate tells you that he took over an existing territory that was significantly below quota and, within three months, the territory was on quota, I would be suspicious. The only possible way this could have occurred is if (A) the territory was not doing as poorly as he has led you to believe, (B) if his predecessor was on the edge of closing several deals that he merely saw to fruition or (C) if he hit what is typically called a "bluebird" or lucky deal.

You know your markets. You know how long it takes to develop a territory. If you are given information that sounds too good to believe, don't! Dig deeper before you assume that a superstar is sitting across the desk from you.

Ferreting out Information

All candidates want to paint themselves in the best light. It is natural that they will only volunteer information that accomplishes that goal. Many interviewers never get into detail during interviews, and candidates, knowing this, will focus only on their successes in a very general way. You must ask enough questions to allow yourself the opportunity to determine if the candidate matches the qualifications listed on the résumé. The following is a typical exchange:

> Interviewer: Tell me, who were your major customers?
> Interviewee: ABC was a major customer of mine. When I took over the territory, we were not doing anything with them. After one year, our annual sales to them was one million dollars.

At this point, an inexperienced interviewer thinks to himself,

> "ABC is a large company. This candidate must be good to have developed this customer into a one million dollar account. This may be my candidate!"

The smart, experienced interviewer never stops there. Unless you get more detail, you will never determine whether the candidate has been altogether up-front. You have to follow up with enough questions to extract specific details about the account's development.

"Who was your initial contact?"
"Who did you deal with in the organization?"
"What was his title?"
"How did you approach the company?"
"Tell me the steps you took to get them to purchase your product."

The answers to these questions will not only give you an idea of the level of the candidate's selling skills, but his account strategies, his persistence, and his ability to overcome obstacles as well. Vague answers to these questions may indicate that the candidate did not make the sales as stated, or that he may have inherited an existing account that was ready to close.

Competition

A good salesperson makes a point of knowing the competition. To effectively place one's product in the best light, one must have an understanding of how it stacks up against similar products in the market. Questions like, "Who was your major competitor?" and "Why do you believe you beat the competition?" can give you a good handle on how knowledgeable a candidate is in this area. I once asked a candidate the last question to which he responded, "We were cheaper." As we reviewed other sales situations, it became apparent that he sold based on price only, and we were looking for someone who knew how to sell benefits.

Territory Management

Organized and efficient territory management and good prospecting skills will be an important factor in determining the future success of any candidate, so you will want to probe this area thoroughly during an interview. A few key questions will give you insight into a candidate's effectiveness in this area. Some suitable questions might be:

"How many customer calls would you say you
   average in a typical day?"
"Where do you get your leads?"

These questions will tell you whether the candidate is getting qualified leads from his company or getting the majority of leads from his own cold calling. If the leads are coming from the company and you need someone who is skilled in cold calling, obviously you may have a mismatch.

Closing Questions

Make it a point to end each interview with the following two questions, geared to offer a glimpse into the personality of each candidate. You would be surprised at the responses.

"What do you consider to be your strengths?"
"What do you perceive your weaknesses are?"
                    or
"In what areas do you feel you could improve?"

Reference Checking

"Sure-Fire" Reference Checks

Most standard reference checks include information taken from the candidate's immediate supervisor, someone who worked for him and a peer of his. If the candidate is still employed and does not wish to reveal his job search, he will usually prefer to refer you to a previous employer.

Here is a "sure-fire" way to run a thorough reference check. In addition to the standard contacts, ask the candidate to supply you with the names of three customers he has sold and three customers with whom he was not successful. And don't just leave it at that. Call them!

I once called a candidate's list of three "good" customers and found two of the three had difficulty remembering who he was. You can imagine what that told me!

Elicit as much information as you can from these customers. They are invaluable sources of information. Short of going out into the field with the salesperson, nothing will offer you a better look into your candidate's skills. Establish how he approached them. What was sold? How long did the sale take? What was their biggest concern? How did the candidate win them over? How often did they see him? What, in their estimation, was the candidate's strength? What were his weaknesses?

The Delicate Probe

As you are aware, most people are hesitant to volunteer negative comments about a business acquaintance. Effective referencing usually requires delicacy and an understanding of this natural reticence. With so much at stake, you need accurate and honest answers to your questions. How do you work around this hesitancy? How do you elicit the information you need without putting the candidate's old customers in a corner?

Perhaps, in the past, you were forced to trust your instincts when making hiring decisions, or tried to read between the lines with regard to the comments you received. Both methods are risky and inaccurate.

Here is a technique that consistently works. Conclude your conversations with a candidate's customers by asking them to spend a moment thinking about the best salesperson with whom they have ever dealt. Ask them to consider that particular salesperson a "10." Follow this by asking them to rank my candidate on a scale of 1 to 10, with 10 being the best.

It is amazing how many times you will hear glowing comments throughout the check, only to have the reference contact respond to this inquiry with a "6" or less. A natural follow-up question is to ask them to share their opinion as to how the candidate might achieve a full "10."

If the consensus is that the individual is an 8, 9, or 10, hire him. A ranking of "7" can be considered marginal, with total dismissal of anyone who consistently falls below that.

These two unique reference techniques have worked time and time again.

BASIC PRINCIPLES

Start out with a good job description.

Share the job description with all interviewers.

Be on the lookout for showstoppers:

- The continuous use of "I"

- Attainment of sales goals in an unrealistic period of time

- Vague answers to questions

When reference checking:

- Ask for 3 customers to whom your prospect has sold and 3 with whom he or she was not successful.

- Ask customers to rank your prospect on a scale of one to ten.

20

SENIOR SALES MANAGEMENT VISITS

The Vice President of Sales is coming to visit! And you know you're going under the microscope. Your palms start to sweat, your knotting stomach turns over, and your heart starts pounding just thinking about it.

In the past, you've handled it like most of your peers. You scurry around gathering data regarding your present revenue status, your key accounts, and your projected sales forecast. You put your staff on alert. You make mental notes of the things you want to tell the vice president if you get the chance, like your upcoming advertising blitz and how you feel sure that it's going to generate a lot of interest in the next six months. Then, right before she arrives, you get down and pray that you'll have everything you need to answer the barrage of questions that she might throw at you. Before you get up, you throw in a little request. "Oh God! Please let her have an early flight out." Am I close?

The first thing we have to change is that poor attitude. Visits from senior management are not doomsday calls. They are opportunities that don't come along very often. They are your chance to excel and distinguish yourself from your peers. You know that your boss has a lot of influence and probably plays a pivotal role in deciding who's promoted or, at the very least, who receives a raise. So, get that "end-of-the-world" attitude out of your head. Replace it with a determination to make this your opportunity.

No one can help you get rid of those wet palms nor can anyone do anything to stop your fluttering heart, but doing so may not be a good idea. This is an important event, and you should be excited. Try these tips on how to turn this visit into your opportunity.

There are two important concepts to keep in mind:

1. You must control the meeting
2. Keep your presentation constructive

Controlling the Meeting

Let's start by remembering the criteria of management regarding promotions. One of the key elements was organization, remember?

"But I am organized!" you cry. "I've compiled all this information."

But what do you plan to do with it? Are you hoping to whip it out when the vice president asks you a question? Surely that would show your organization and impress her, right? But will you even be able to find it with those trembling hands? Probably not! If you expect to appear organized, you've got to do better than that. Finding the information in response to her questions is a reactionary response and is not to be confused with preparation. To appear prepared and organized, you are going to have to control the meeting. To control the meeting, you will have to a have a set agenda and a focused presentation.

With these, you are in the driver's seat. With these, you needn't worry about so many of those random questions that have a tendency to throw you.

Your presentation should be on an overhead projector or on a flip chart. The following is an example of how your presentation might open:

Sales Manager–

"I appreciate the opportunity to review what we've been doing. I realize that your time is limited, and I want to make your visit as productive as possible. I've put together some material on our district. Let's take a look at the objectives and topics I thought you might want to cover."

(The following objectives are for the purpose of demonstration, but might prove useful as a guide.)

OBJECTIVES

• To update you on the revenue status of the district
  • Where we are today
  • Where we plan to be by year's end
  • How we plan to get there

• To discuss a number of district and company problems/issues and recommend solutions

• To review areas where we can use your support to aid us in achieving our revenue objectives

(Overhead #1)

Sales Manager–

"In order to fully meet these objectives, I planned to cover the following topics:"

AGENDA

A. Territory Overview
   1. Sales Territory Overview
     • Largest Companies
     • Largest Existing Customers
     • Major Competitive Accounts

   2. Year-To-Date Revenue vs. Forecast
     • Reasons for Differences

   3. Forecast for Remainder of Year
     • Assumptions
     • Forecast

B. Revenue Stimulation Programs
   1. Goals and Objectives
   2. Sales Tactics
   3. Customer Plans

C. Inhibitors to Meeting Revenue Objectives
   1. Product Issues
   2. Sales Issues
   3. Corporate Issues
   4. Other Issues

(Overhead #2)

Your presentation should be formatted in much the same way as territory plans, which were discussed in detail in Chapter 2. This presentation is merely a compilation of the individual plans of your salespeople.

Once the agenda is presented, it is important to ask the vice president if she thinks it will cover the material in which she was interested. If she responds by adding a topic that was not specifically listed, don't get flustered. You can incorporate the topic into your presentation. Consider where her request could be covered, if it is not already in your presentation, and continue. The one thing you do not want to do is get sidetracked before you begin. Any one of the following types of statements should be enough to keep things on track:

"Why don't I cover that as part of the Customer Plans?"
"I had planned to cover that as part of the discussion of key accounts."
"Why don't I cover that after Revenue Stimulation Programs?"

These responses keep your presentation intact, maintain your control over the meeting and, most importantly, buy you time to respond.

Keep Your Presentation Constructive

The presentation of your Inhibitors to Meeting Revenue Objectives (See C - Overhead #2) requires delicacy and finesse. While it is important to state your concerns clearly and concisely, it is even more important that you voice them in a professional way that will encourage the formulation of workable solutions and answers to the problems.

As a general manager and vice president, I have seen many presentations deteriorate when these issues are discussed. Good, informative presentations can suddenly become nothing more than 'gripe sessions' that leave the senior manager or vice president with a truly sour taste for the entire presentation. This is unfortunate since the judicious introduction of these issues can do much to advance a sales manager's reputation as that "All Important Problem Solver."

Product Issues

As you well know, product inhibitors are an especially irritating source of frustration to salespeople and their managers. Recurring software glitches, chronic hardware malfunctions, delays with product introduction, or any number of service problems present major obstacles to the sales organization's ability to sell. However, these issues can be discussed and dealt with in a tactful and productive manner.

Let's look at two different sales managers' approaches to presenting these concerns to upper management. Make note of the very different perceptions that are left following each of the presentations.

> Sales Manager #1: Sally, we are still having problems with the software in Product A. It's killing us! More customers are complaining every day. We're having to spend half of our days with our existing customers. How can my staff be expected to make our revenue unless this is fixed immediately?

Does this sales manager really believe that Sally is not aware of the magnitude of the problem? This sales manager certainly makes it sound that way. Big Mistake! Of course, Sally is aware of this! In all likelihood, she has spent a lot of time dealing with this very issue.

Not only does he make an erroneous assumption, but he follows by presenting a veiled threat. "If you don't fix this right now, I won't be held accountable for my revenue!" He sounds like he is already anticipating failure and beginning to gather his excuses.

Now let's look at how Sales Manager #2 presents the very same problem:

> Sales Manager #2: As you are aware, the problems with Product A are impacting our sales and hurting our cred-

ibility with existing customers. Do you have any idea when we might expect a solution to the software problem? Is there anything you could suggest that we tell the customers that are calling in?

This Sales Manager assumes that Sally is doing her job and is aware of the software problem. If for some unknown reason, Sally was not up-to-date, this manager wisely assumes that she will ask him to elaborate on what is going on. He tactfully states the problem and immediately turns the attention to finding a solution. He uses words like "we" and "our" and takes a partner-like approach to finding a solution. Unlike Sales Manager #1, it is clear that he expects that there will be a resolution in the foreseeable future. He elicits Sally's suggestions to help him get through the interim.

Let's carry the discussion further. Let's assume that Sally has assured both sales managers that the problem will be sorted out within sixty days. How does each react to this news?

> Sales Manager #1: Good! I hope this is the end of it. It seems like every time we turn around there's another glitch. Can't we get quality control personnel that will catch these things before we turn the product over to the customers? Or better yet, can't we get engineers that know how to design the products in the first place?

Sales Manager #1 should be voted "Pessimist of the Year." It is clear that he has no confidence in either the company's ability to solve the problem or in the visiting manager either. He hints that he does not believe that the problem has really been solved and goes on to double dump on quality control and the engineering department. This dumping is very poorly timed since he has just received assurances that they are close to correcting the problem. He clearly demonstrates his feeling that it's "us" against "them."

In addition, it is obvious that he has never learned the graciousness of a "Thank You" and does absolutely nothing to ingratiate himself with Sally.

Sales Manager #2 takes a different approach:

"That's a load off my mind. I know my people will be glad to hear that. In the interim, should we be looking at a containment strategy? What would you think if I assigned Joe to the office full-time to handle customer calls just until this is all ironed out. He's technically strong and works well with customers. I believe this one point of contact would be helpful and signal to the customers that we are as concerned as they are. I also plan to visit our top ten customers in the next two weeks to reassure them. I know they'll be happy about your news."

Sales Manager #2 exudes confidence, not only in his company, but in his management as well. He once again shows his team spirit. He appears eager to share the news with his people and is ready to involve himself in a strategy to contain problems. It is also obvious that he has spent some time thinking about a solution to the problem prior to Sally's visit. He displays confidence in Joe as he sets out his plans to reassure his customers.

Here is the same problem handled two very different ways. Is there any question who would come out shining and who effectively buried himself in a heap of complaints?

Sales Issues

Sales Issues present you with an opportunity to discuss any specific personnel problems or the need for additional sales or product training programs. If you have reservations regarding a particular employee, state these as professionally and dispassionately as possible and your plan of action to correct the problem.

Corporate Issues

Corporate issues can be every bit as troublesome as product issues. Delivery problems (short shipments, late shipments) and poor response times from the corporation (with proposals, pricing issues, technical questions, competitive information etc,) can be real showstoppers. As before, the sales manager needs to articulate the problems, but must be mindful of how he does so.

As before, it may be helpful to show how one problem can be articulated by two very different people:

> Sales Manager #1: We just released Product B and, as usual, all we got was a product brochure. There was no competitive information or detailed explanations on the features and benefits. Why do we keep making the same mistake? How can I expect my salespeople to sell the product without this kind of information?

> Sales Manager #2: I'm pleased to see that new products are coming out. We just got the product brochures on Product B, and my group is eager to get started plugging it. However, we didn't receive any information regarding competitive products or any explanations on the features and benefits we will be pushing with it. As you are aware, this has been a recurring problem.
>
> I've asked Mary to talk to Wayne at the corporate office. She's trying to get as much material as she can to present at our next sales meeting. She's doing a good job of pulling it together, but I know that the information corporate could supply is a lot more polished and professional. Is there anything you could do to facilitate this process? Any help you could give us would be appreciated. We really want to seize the moment when products are released.

Once again, it is obvious that Sales Manager #1 has only used this part of his presentation to grumble about "his" problems, where the Sales Manager #2 has stated his concerns, and gone a step further to position himself as a problem solver. While he recognizes shortcomings, he presents himself as someone who is trying to stay on "top of things" and operate within the controls that are given to him. Which of the two would you consider for promotion?

In summary, a presentation to a senior manager or vice president is an opportunity that does not come along very often. The impression you leave may very well determine your standing in the company for some time to come. At the risk of being redundant, be prepared, be clear and concise, and be professional.

BASIC PRINCIPLES

To be successful during senior management visits you must:

- Be prepared

- Control the meeting

- Keep your presentation constructive

21

EPILOGUE

Marshall Field in Chicago was one of the first of the high-class big-city department stores to get into trouble in the 1970s—and one of the first ones to get out of trouble too. Three or four consecutive CEOs tried to change the culture—to no avail. Then a new CEO came in who asked "What do we have to produce by the way of results?" Every one of his store managers knew the answer. "We have to increase the amount each shopper spends per visit." Then he asked, "Do any of our stores actually do this?" Three or four—out of 30 or so—actually did it. "Will you then tell us," the new CEO asked, "what you people do that gives you the desired results?"

In every single case these results were achieved not by doing something different but by systematically doing something everyone had known all along should be done, had in the policy manuals, and had been preaching—but only the few exceptions had been practicing."[16]

As Marshall Field discovered and every Top Performer knows, it is not always the new or novel approach that ensures success. Many times, it is one's adherence to the tried and true methods that make sense.

In this book, we have illustrated the tried and true methods that have consistently led to the success of Top

[16]Peter F. Drucker, *Managing for the Future* (New York: Truman Talley Books/Dutton, 1992), p. 194.

Performers. If you incorporate the tried and true ideas suggested in this book into your everyday activities, you too can become a Top Performer. You too will succeed in the competitive '90s. Good luck!

APPENDIX

SAMPLE TERRITORY PLAN

SAMPLE TERRITORY PLAN

Author's Note: We will assume that this plan, which is for a fictitious data communications company called Caliber Inc., was prepared in August for presentation in September. Therefore, at the time of preparation, this year's total territory sales figures were not known.

Explanations of the various components will only be included when needed.

A. Sales Territory Overview

1. Largest Cities

The territory consists of two states, Kentucky and Tennessee with populations of 3.7 million and 4.8 million, respectively. The table below shows all cities with a population of more than 50,000.

City	Population (000)	%
Kentucky		
Louisville	294	7.9
Lexington	214	5.8
Owensboro	56	1.6
Tennessee		
Memphis	646	13.4
Nashville	456	9.5
Knoxville	175	3.6
Chattanooga	170	3.5
Clarksville	55	1.1

2. Number of Companies by Market Segment

There are approximately 232 companies with annual revenue of more than 100 million dollars. They are broken into the following categories:

Number	Category
18	Wholesale trade
17	Electric services
15	Food products
11	Coal mining
10	Miscellaneous manufacturing
8	Food stores
6	Petroleum
	etc.

(A detailed list of customers by Standard Industrial Classifications is shown in Exhibit A.)

Author's Note: Too often salespeople try to sell all the large companies in their area. I am a strong believer in market segmentation. Focus on those market segments whose customers have business problems that your product best solves. This approach allows you to maximize your revenue while minimizing your time and expenses. You will see how this principle is applied in Section C of the Sample Territory Plan.

3. Largest Companies

The 10 largest companies follows. Other companies (with revenue over 100 million dollars) are shown in Exhibit B, in descending order.

Ten Largest Companies

Company	Market Segment	City/State	Revenue (000,000)
Ashland Oil Inc.	Petroleum	Russell, KY	9,923
Federal Express Corp.	Transportation	Memphis, TN	7,688
Kentucky Fried Chicken Corp.	Eating places	Louisville, KY	6,000
Humana Inc.	Health services	Louisville, KY	5,865
Tennessee Valley Authority	Electric services	Knoxville, TN	5,136
Hospital Corp. of America	Health services	Nashville, TN	4,631
Service Merchandise Company	General merchandise	Brentwood, TN	3,435
Malone & Hyde Inc.	Wholesale trade	Memphis, TN	3,086
Batus Holding Inc.	Tobacco products	Louisville, KY	2,900
Ingram Industries Inc.	Water transportation	Memphis, TN	2,676

4. Largest Existing Caliber Customers

Customer	Type Business	This Year's Anticipated Sales (000)
Federal Express Inc.	Transportation	120
Humana Inc.	Health services	88
Service Merchandise Company	General merchandise	65
Embassy Suites Inc.	Hotels	43
Brown-Forman Corp.	Food products	40
Ashland Oil Inc.	Petroleum	40
Tennessee Valley Authority	Electric services	36
TBC Corp.	Wholesale trade	35
Red Food Stores Inc.	Food stores	22
Arco Aluminum Inc.	Wholesale trade	15
Total		504
This Year's Expected Revenue		1,200
Top 10 as a % of total sales		42%

The figures above show the anticipated business from our top 10 customers this year. We anticipate closing this year on quota, which is 1.2 million. Therefore, our top 10 customers will have accounted for 42% of our revenue.

5. Major Competitive Accounts

Our two major competitors are the DEF Company and the ABC Company. By far, DEF is the stronger of the two. They have an experienced sales organization and product features that match ours. They tend to price competitively, particularly on large potential orders. The following are the major accounts signed by our competitors.

Competitor	Company
DEF Company	Malone & Hyde Inc.
DEF Company	Hospital Corporation of America
DEF Company	Thomas Industries Inc.
ABC Company	Batus Holding Inc.
ABC Company	Kentucky Utilities Company Inc.
ABC Company	Texas Gas Transmission Corp.

B. Next Year's Sales Forecast

1. Forecast Assumptions

a. $270,000 of my forecast is based on new product availability. In order to meet this new product forecast, it is assumed that we will have Product A available for testing by our customers by November 15th and that Product B will be available for customer tests by May 15th. We have already identified those customers that are interested in these products. Any delay in product availability will understandably impact next year's revenue.

b. It is assumed that our Vice President of Sales will be available to make executive visit calls to my top five customers in December and January.

c. It is also assumed that direct mail brochures will be ready for customer distribution by January 5th.

Author's Note: Too often, salespeople fail to list the assumptions upon which their forecasts are based. This is a major omission. If the forecasts are missed, the salespeople are usually blamed, regardless of the circumstances that may have been beyond their control.

This is frequently the case with new products. Forecasts are routinely made based on assumptions that the new products will be are routinely available for sale on given dates. But as we all know, new product introduction dates have a way of slipping. Unfortunately, our forecasts are not easily forgotten and we are held accountable for the revenue, product or not. When we come up short, no one seems to remember that Product XYZ was five months late coming off the production line.

I once worked for a General Manager who did not appreciate the impact that late availability of new products had on forecasts. Prior to our fiscal year, I changed the way I submitted and tracked new products. In addition to developing a forecast by customer (which included new product sales), I set up a separate category called "New Products" (See B. 3 New Product Forecast). I then listed these new products by availability dates and tracked them on a separate forecast. My point was made when the revenue shortfall for that year was two million dollars, the exact number forecasted for the new products that failed to make it off the drawing boards.

One division of a multi-billion dollar company no longer includes new products in their revenue forecasts unless they are available at the time the forecast is prepared. They had been "burned" too many times in the past.

2. Next Year's Forecast

Customer	Type Business	Next Year's Revenue Forecast (000)				
		1st Qtr.	2nd Qtr.	3rd Qtr.	4th Qtr.	Total
Existing Customers						
Federal Express Inc.	Transportation	40	40	55	70	205
Humana Inc.	Health services	50	25	0	0	75
Service Merchandise Company	General merch.	25	30	40	20	115
Embassy Suites Inc.	Hotels	25	25	25	25	100
Brown-Forman Corp.	Food products	40	30	25	10	105
Ashland Oil Inc.	Petroleum	10	10	10	25	55
Tennessee Valley Authority	Electric services	20	20	10	25	75
TBC Corp.	Wholesale trade	5	10	10	20	45
Red Food Stores Inc.	Food stores	5	5	5	5	20
Arco Aluminum Inc.	Wholesale trade	10	0	20	0	30

2. Next Year's Forecast (cont.)

Customer	Type Business	Next Year's Revenue Forecast (000)				
		1st Qtr.	2nd Qtr.	3rd Qtr.	4th Qtr.	Total
Existing Customers—New Opportunities						
Ashland Oil Inc.	Petroleum	15	20	25	25	85
Pilot Corp.	Automotive	10	20	20	20	70
Dairyman Inc.	Wholesale trade	0	10	20	0	30
Others		40	40	50	45	175
Total Existing Customers		295	285	315	290	1185
New Business						
Autozone Inc.	Automotive	10	20	30	25	85
Island Creek Corp.	Coal mining	20	20	20	20	80
McKee Foods Corp.	Food products	0	25	25	25	75
Others		15	20	25	25	85
Total New Business		45	85	100	95	325
Total Forecast—Next Year		340	370	415	385	1510
3. New Product Forecast						
Product A.		20	40	60	80	200
Product B.		0	10	20	40	70
Total		20	50	80	120	270

Author's Note: Your forecast should be by the month. In this sample it was shown by the quarter for ease of presentation. Many companies like to look at a two year forecast. In that situation, the second year would be forecasted by the quarter.

C. Next Year's Revenue Stimulation Plans

Author's Note: This is the heart of your territory plan. It describes, in detail, your plans for attaining your revenue goals. As stated earlier, your goals and objectives state what you want to achieve, your strategies are how you plan to do it, and your tactics are what you plan to do.

This section should be modified as market conditions and competitive factors change. It should be considered a working document, which will keep you on track if you refer to it regularly. Too often we tend to forget what we set out to accomplish as we get involved in the day-to-day details of our job. After ignoring their plans for months salespeople are often surprised to find that many of their planned activities were never implemented.

1. Goals and Objectives

Achieve a revenue objective of 1.5 million dollars, a 25 percent increase over this year's anticipated revenue of 1.2 million.

2. Strategies

a. Focus on those market segments that:
  • we have had the most success with, because our product has features that provide benefits to their specific business problems.

  • historically spend money for data communications to solve their business problems.

b. Increase revenue from our existing customer base by introducing and selling our new products.

c. Sign at least one existing competitive account.

d. Use seminars:
- to increase sales from existing small and medium accounts by 6 percent.

- to sign new small and medium accounts.

e. Maintain existing base by:
- setting up executive visits with my top five accounts in December and January.

- reviewing my account plans for the upcoming year with my top ten customers.

f. Increase sales productivity by increasing the number of face-to-face visits per month by eight.

3. General Tactics

a. Focus on those market segments with which we have had the most success with and those that have the highest expenditures for data communications.

Based on these criteria, I plan to focus on the following segments:

Segment	# of Companies (Sales Over 100 M)
Wholesale trade	18
Electric services	17
Food products	15
Eating places	8
Petroleum	6

I plan to set up visits with all companies in these segments that I have not seen to date. These companies can be found in Exhibit A. Further, my seminar program for small and medium companies will initially focus on these segments.

b. Increase revenue from our existing customer base by introducing and selling our new products.

Our best source of revenue for our new products comes from our existing base. I have already introduced Product A to our top ten customers and four of them have agreed to test the product. A successful test will result in fore-casted orders. I plan to closely monitor these test sites over the initial sixty-day period. John (our technical support person) will call each site every other day for the first two weeks and then once a week. I plan to call each site at least weekly and to visit each one within the first month of the test.

I am presently identifying other customers or potential customers who could use this product. This list will be completed by October 15th.

c. Sign at least one existing competitive account.

I plan to focus on the competitive accounts of ABC Company, since they are the weaker competitor and do not have all the user-features of our products. My plan is to call on their three major customers as identified in A.5.

4. Seminar Program

In order to reach my medium and small accounts effectively, I plan to run one seminar per quarter. The seminars will be held in the following cities:

City	Month
Memphis	March
Louisville	June
Nashville	September
Lexington	December

5. Maintain Existing Base

I plan to set up executive visits with the Vice President of Sales and my five major accounts in December and January. The visit schedule will be confirmed by October 15th. I plan to use this opportunity to review my account plans for them and gain their concurrence.

6. Increase sales productivity by increasing the number of face-to-face visits per month by eight.

I plan to accomplish this by setting aside one-half day a week specifically for "cold calling."

7. Specific Tactics/Programs

December
- Set up visits with eight of the companies in the targeted market segments.
- Finalize test plans for Product A, with the four companies (Ashland Oil Inc., Tennessee Valley Authority, Island Creek Corp., Embassy Suites Inc.) testing the product.

- Set up times for our technical support person and me to call to get updates on product test results.
- Set a date in the beginning of January for formal review of the test and to discuss the product order.
- Conduct key customer visits with the Vice President of Sales.
- Identify the names of medium and small companies in targeted segments to invite to the first seminar.

January
- Set up visits with another eight of the companies in the targeted market segments.
- Set a seminar date and pick a hotel for the first product seminar to be held in Memphis.
- Set up visits and a presentation of Product A to those top twenty customers who have not seen the product.
- Complete key customer visits with the Vice President of Sales.

February
- Set up visits to ABC's three major accounts.
- Mail seminar invitations (to be mailed 30 days prior to seminar).
- Telephone follow-up for all invited guests 10 days prior to seminar.

March
- Set up visits with another eight of the companies in the targeted market segments.
- Re-evaluate the status of Product A. Determine additional product introduction strategies.
- Develop plans for introduction of Product B.

8. Customer Plans

Author's Note: The following section gives a brief overview of the opportunities that are possible for each forecasted customer.

Existing Customers

> Company: Service Merchandise Company
> Application: Customer service
> Forecast: $115,000
> Product(s): 10 Controllers/80 CRT's
> Probability of Success: 90 percent
> Comments: Service Merchandise Company has been a customer of ours since 1986. Based on forecasted growth by them of their customer service application, they anticipate ordering an additional 10 controllers and 80 CRT's. See KAAP for detail account plan.

(A discussion of other existing customers that appear in the forecast that were not discussed at other points in the review would follow.)

Existing Customers—New Opportunities

> Company: Ashland Oil Inc.
> Application: Inventory control
> Forecast: $85,000
> Product(s): 8 Controllers/64 CRT's
> Probability of Success: 70 percent
> Comments: Ashland has been testing 3 CRT's and 1 controller in a warehouse application that tracks inventory in and out of the warehouse. The order is dependent on whether Ashland can maintain accu-

rate inventory records with this system. We have been working closely with them, and initial results are encouraging. DEF Company is our major competitor. The KAAP details our strategy and discusses the competitive situation in detail.

(A discussion of other existing customers who present new opportunities would follow.)

New Business

> Company: Autozone Inc.
> Application: Parts inventory
> Forecast: $85,000
> Product(s): 6 Controllers/64 CRT's/64 Wand readers
> Probability of Success: 60 percent
> Comments: Autozone has successfully completed testing the use of bar codes to keep track of its parts inventory. Vendor selection for this project is between the DEF Company and Caliber. A decision is scheduled for December with initial deliveries to begin in March. The customer is pleased with our response in modifying our software to accept multiple check digits. DEF cannot do this in their equipment, which gives us the inside track. They need exposure to our company, and I believe a meeting with top management will make them feel more comfortable purchasing from our company. My plan is to invite their Vice President of Engineering, who is the decision maker, and the two decision influencers, Tom and Pete, to our facility in November for a plant tour and a visit with our president.

(A discussion of other new business accounts that appear in the forecast would follow.)

D. Inhibitors for Meeting Revenue Objectives

Author's Note: This section is concerned with those issues that stand in the way or keep you from achieving your revenue objective. Inhibitors may be broadly defined as any issues that may have a significant, negative impact on your revenue objectives such as product, sales or corporate issues.

Inhibitors could be:

A well-entrenched competitor
Stiffer competition in the pricing area
A lack of technical support
A key feature that is missing
Late delivery dates

Exhibit A

Companies with Annual Revenues
Greater than 100 Million

Listed by Standard Industrial Classifications

Company	City & State	Revenue (000,000)
SIC #1211—Bituminous Coal and Lignite Mining		
Island Creek Corp.	Lexington, KY	694
Addington Resources Inc.	Ashland, Ky	269
Coal-Mac Inc.	Pikeville, KY	151
etc.		
SIC # 4911—Electric Services		
Tennessee Valley Authority	Knoxville, TN	5,136
LG&E Energy Corp.	Louisville, KY	698
Louisville Gas & Electric System	Louisville, KY	689
etc.		
SIC # 5812—Eating Places		
Kentucky Fried Chicken Corp.	Louisville, KY	6,000
Jerrico Inc.	Lexington, KY	635
Chi-Chi's USA Inc.	Lexington, KY	363
etc.		

The remainder of the companies would be listed by SIC codes.

Exhibit B

Companies with Annual Revenues
Greater than 100 Million

Company	Market Segment	City/State	Revenue (000,000)
Toyota Motor USA Inc.	Transportation equip.	Georgetown, KY	2,500
Eastman Chemical Products Inc.	Wholesale trade	Kingsport, TN	2,200
Martin Marietta Energy Systems Inc.	Engineering services	Oak Ridge, TN	2,200

The remainder of the companies in descending order would follow.